Illinois Central College
Learning Resource Center

EGLI

THE WEEK-END BOOK OF HUMOR

The
WEEK-END BOOK
of HUMOR

Selected by
P. G. WODEHOUSE, 1881-
and SCOTT MEREDITH

General Introduction by Mr. Wodehouse
Introductions to Selections by Mr. Meredith

Essay Index Reprint Series

BOOKS FOR LIBRARIES PRESS
FREEPORT, NEW YORK

Copyright 1952 by P. G. Wodehouse and Scott Meredith

Reprinted 1971 by arrangement with
Scott Meredith Literary Agency

INTERNATIONAL STANDARD BOOK NUMBER:
0-8369-2094-5

LIBRARY OF CONGRESS CATALOG CARD NUMBER:
71-134162

PRINTED IN THE UNITED STATES OF AMERICA

Acknowledgments

"Take the Witness!" by Robert Benchley, copyright, 1936, by Robert C. Benchley, is reprinted by permission of Harper and Brothers from *My Ten Years in a Quandary*.

"Groucho: The Man from Marx" by Leo Rosten, copyright, 1950, by Cowles Magazines, Inc., appeared originally in *Look* Magazine. Reprinted by permission of the author.

"Somewhere a Roscoe . . ." by S. J. Perelman, copyright, 1938, by S. J. Perelman, which appeared originally in *The New Yorker* Magazine, is reprinted by permission of Random House, Inc., from *Crazy Like a Fox*.

"Father Wakes Up the Village" by Clarence Day, copyright, 1934, 1935, by Clarence Day, is reprinted by permission of Alfred A. Knopf, Inc., from *Life with Father*.

"Song to Be Sung by the Father of Infant Female Children" by Ogden Nash, copyright, 1933, by Ogden Nash, is reprinted by permission of Little, Brown and Company from *Many Long Years Ago*.

"Capsule Criticism" by Alexander Woollcott, copyright, 1946, by The Viking Press, Inc., is reprinted by permission of The Viking Press, Inc., from *The Portable Alexander Woollcott*.

"Two Bums Here Would Spend Freely Except for Poverty" by John McNulty, copyright, 1941, 1942, 1943, 1944, 1946, by John McNulty, is reprinted by permission of Little, Brown and Company from *Third Avenue, New York*.

"The Snatching of Bookie Bob" by Damon Runyon, copyright, 1931, 1932, 1933, 1934, by Damon Runyon, is reprinted by permission of the J. B. Lippincott Company from *Blue Plate Special*.

"Thoughts" by John O'Reilly, copyright, 1952, by John O'Reilly. Reprinted by permission of the author.

"Yvonne" by Frank Sullivan, copyright, 1933, by Frank Sullivan, is reprinted by permission of The Viking Press, Inc., from *In One Ear*.

"Adventures with the Angels" by H. Allen Smith, copyright, 1943, by H. Allen Smith, is reprinted by permission of Doubleday and Company, Inc., from *Life in a Putty Knife Factory*.

"Twenty-Five by Cerf" by Bennett Cerf, copyright, 1945, by Bennett Cerf, appeared originally in *Laughing Stock*, published by Grosset and Dunlap. Reprinted by permission of the author.

"Chocolate for the Woodwork" by Arthur Kober, copyright, 1941, by Arthur Kober, is reprinted by permission of Random House, Inc., from *My Dear Bella*.

"Résumé" by Dorothy Parker, copyright, 1926, 1944, by Dorothy Parker, is reprinted by permission of The Viking Press, Inc., from *The Portable Dorothy Parker*.

vi   *Acknowledgments*

"Love Is a Fallacy" by Max Shulman, copyright, 1951, by Max Shulman, is reprinted by permission of Doubleday and Company, Inc., from *The Many Loves of Dobie Gillis.*

"The Lady on the Bookcase" by James Thurber, copyright, 1931, 1932, 1934, 1935, 1936, 1937, 1945, by James Thurber. Reprinted by permission of the author.

"New Joe Miller Joke Book" by Earl Wilson, copyright, 1945, by Earl Wilson, is reprinted by permission of Doubleday and Company, Inc., from *I Am Gazing Into My 8-Ball.*

"On the Vanity of Earthly Greatness" by Arthur Guiterman, copyright, 1936, by E. P. Dutton & Co., Inc., is reprinted by permission of E. P. Dutton & Co., Inc., from *Gaily the Troubadour.*

"The Etiquette of Courtship" by Donald Ogden Stewart, copyright, 1922, by Doubleday and Company, Inc., is reprinted by permission of Doubleday and Company, Inc., and the author, from *Perfect Behavior.*

"Confetti on the Brain" by Billy Rose, copyright, 1946, by Glenmore Productions, Inc., is reprinted by permission of Simon and Schuster, Publishers, from *Wine, Women and Words.*

"Madame Du Barry" by Will Cuppy, copyright, 1950, by Fred Feldkamp, is reprinted by permission of Henry Holt and Company, Inc., from *The Decline and Fall of Practically Everybody.*

"Money" by Richard Armour, copyright, 1942, by Richard Armour, is reprinted by permission of Bruce Humphries, Inc., from *Yours for the Asking.*

"Herr Otto Brauhaus" by Ludwig Bemelmans, copyright, 1938, by Ludwig Bemelmans, is reprinted by permission of The Viking Press, Inc., from *Life Class;* now included in *Hotel Bemelmans.*

"Guinea Pig" by Ruth McKenney, copyright, 1938, by Ruth McKenney, is reprinted by permission of Harcourt, Brace and Company, Inc., from *My Sister Eileen.*

The Man Who Came to Dinner by George S. Kaufman and Moss Hart, copyright, 1939, by George S. Kaufman and Moss Hart, is reprinted by permission of Random House, Inc., from *The Man Who Came to Dinner.*

"Trouble Down at Tudsleigh" by P. G. Wodehouse, copyright, 1925, 1926, 1928, 1931, 1935, 1937, 1939, 1940, by Pelham Grenville Wodehouse, appeared originally in *Eggs, Beans and Crumpets,* published by Doubleday and Company, Inc. Reprinted by permission of the author and his agents, the Scott Meredith Literary Agency.

Cartoons by Henry Sylverson, Mort Walker, Tom Hudson, Salo Roth, Jeff Keate, and Ernest Marquez appeared originally in *The Saturday Evening Post,* and are reprinted by permission of *The Saturday Evening Post* and the artists. All cartoons are copyright by The Curtis Publishing Company, under the following dates: Sylverson, 1949; Walker, 1949; Hudson, 1947; Roth, 1950; Keate, 1938; Marquez, 1951.

The cartoon by Don Tobin appeared originally in *The American Magazine,* and is reprinted by permission of *The American Magazine* and Mr. Tobin. Copyright, 1947, by the Crowell-Collier Publishing Corporation.

Acknowledgments

Cartoons by Al Ross, Vip (Virgil Partch), Irwin Caplan, and Syd Hoff appeared originally in *Collier's*, and are reprinted by permission of *Collier's* and the artists. All cartoons are copyright by the Crowell-Collier Publishing Corporation, under the following dates: Ross, 1939; Partch, 1943; Caplan, 1951; Hoff, 1948.

Cartoons by Charles Addams, Richard Decker, George Price, Robert Day, and R. Taylor appeared originally in *The New Yorker* Magazine, and are reprinted by permission of *The New Yorker* Magazine and the artists. All cartoons are copyright by *The New Yorker* Magazine, Inc., under the following dates: Addams, 1947; Decker, 1936; Price, 1941; Day, 1944; Taylor, 1939.

Cartoons by Mischa Richter, Roy L. Fox, and Clyde Lamb appeared originally in *This Week* Magazine, and are reprinted by permission of *This Week* Magazine and the artists. All cartoons are copyright by United Newspapers Magazine Corporation under the following dates: Richter, 1942; Fox, 1950; Lamb, 1951.

CONTENTS

Contents

THE WEEK-END BOOK OF HUMOR

INTRODUCTION

MR. CHAIRMAN, ladies and gentlemen.

Seeing your vacant faces and gazing into your fishy eyes as I rise to introduce this book, I am reminded of a little story that may be new to some of you here tonight. But as it is bound to have appeared in the collected works of Bennett Cerf, I will omit it and get down to business.

This is an anthology of the writings of humorists, and the great advantage of publishing an anthology of the writings of humorists is that it brings a ray of sunshine into the poor devils' drab lives. It makes them feel that it is not such a bad little world, after all, and they pour their shot of strychnine back into the bottle. The pleasant shock of finding that somebody loves them revives them like watered flowers. It is so seldom that anyone encourages humorists. I shouldn't wonder if our letter to—say—H. Allen Smith, saying how much we liked his "Adventures with the Angels" and could we use it, was not the first kind word he had had since 1937.

For humorists today are not popular pets. I don't know if you have ever seen someone looking askance at something, but that is how the modern public looks at the authors of what is known in the trade as "light writing." In some states, I believe, it is legal to hunt them with dogs, and even in more humane localities they are scorned and sneered at. I happen to know that the fellow who wrote "Trouble Down at Tudsleigh" at the end of this book was referred to the other day in *The New Yorker* as a "burbling pixie." Well, you can't go calling a man a burbling pixie without lowering his morale. He frets. He refuses to eat his cereal. He goes about with his hands in his pockets and his underlip sticking out, kicking stones. The next thing you know, he has given up humor and is writing thoughtful novels analyzing social conditions, like the author of "When Willie Came to Say Good Night" in George Ade's fable.

The fact of the matter is, America is suffering from a touch of liver. "Never," says a writer in an evening paper, "have I heard so much complaining as I have heard this year. Everybody's got a beef. Never have I seen people so serious, so lacking in spontaneous gaiety, so short of a sense of humor. It was the year of the tart temper, the strident voice, the frustrated desperation." Comedy does not flourish in such an atmosphere, and the humorist, with everyone yelling at him and bullying him, becomes discouraged. "My last month's mail," says Robert C. Ruark in the *World-Telegram*, "has contained outraged yelps on pieces concerning baseball, dogs, diets, cigar-smoking ladies, ulcers, Texas airplanes, cats and kings. I write a piece laughing about the modern tendency to cry, musically, and you would have thought I had assaulted womanhood."

The whole trouble is, as Ruth McKenney puts it, a humorist, in order to be a humorist, must see the world out of focus, yet it is just when the world is really out of focus that people want you to see it straight. Humor implies criticism of established institutions, and nowadays the country is trying to keep its faith in the established order intact. I don't know what is to be done about it. It is what the French would call an impasse. As a matter of fact, it is what the French *do* call an impasse. Only they say anh-parsse. Silly, of course, but you know what Frenchmen are.

Frank Sullivan—I seem always to be writing about

Frank Sullivan— Hi, Frank!—had an article on humor in a recent *New York Times* Book Review so profound, so lucid and well expressed, that I propose to pinch most of it and pass it off as my own. Where, the Sage of Saratoga asked, are the young humorists? Of humorists who were with us in 1920, he says, these have departed—George Ade, Robert Benchley, Will Cuppy, Clarence Day, Finlay Peter Dunne, Will Rogers, Oliver Herford, Ring Lardner, Don Marquis, Booth Tarkington, Thorne Smith, Ellis Parker Butler, Bert Leston Taylor, Harry Leon Wilson, Irvin S. Cobb, Kin Hubbard, Stephen Leacock, Carolyn Wells, George S. Chappell, Roark Bradford, and Gelett Burgess. And where are their successors? His theory is that they are all writing gags for television. If they are, they're lousy. (Specimen, which got through at me last night before I could switch the thing off:

> SHE: You're selfish.
> He: How dare you call me a shellfish?)

It is not difficult to understand any reluctance a young writer might feel toward undertaking the writing of care-free humor today. In the 1920's humorists about to be humorous were not in danger of being stopped dead in their tracks by coming across a photograph of Gromyko or Senator McCarthy. The feeling exists that there is a suspicion of reproach in writing humor now, and some humorists have tried to alibi themselves against this by putting a Message of Social Significance into their humor. Other humorists just give up and join an advertising agency.

(No, it's hopeless to try to pass off anything as good as the above as my own. It is lifted bodily from Le Sullivan.)

To any bright young man with a gift for light writing who is thinking of giving up and joining an advertising agency

I would say "Don't do it, boy. Keep the torch burning. The world may not know it, but it needs humor." No doubt many writers of humor do feel edgy about seeming frivolous these days. No man wants to be accused of laughing, or of being *particeps criminis* to laughter in others, during a wake. Yet people have laughed during wakes before this; in fact, that is one reason why wakes were invented.

(There's that man again. I'm sorry, Frank, but you ought not to tempt a fellow by writing such good stuff.)

When I first came to America—April 25, 1904, now a national holiday—everyone was lighthearted and funny. There were about twenty papers then, morning and evening, and each had its team of humorists turning out daily masterpieces in prose and verse. A magazine like *The Saturday Evening Post* had two funny short stories and a comic article in every number. Publishers published humorous books. It was the golden age, and I think it ought to be brought back. It only needs a little resolution on the part of the young writers and a touch of the old broad-mindedness among editors.

I want to see a Benchley on every street corner, a Harry Leon Wilson in every drugstore.

And if any young writer with a gift for comedy has got the idea that there is something undignified about making people laugh, let him read this from the Talmud, a book which, one may remind him, was written in an age just as grim as this one:

. . . and Elijah said to R. Berokah, these two will also share in the World to Come. R. Berokah then asked them "What is your occupation?" "We are merry-makers; when we see a person who is downcast we cheer him up." . . . These two were of the very select few who would inherit the Kingdom of Heaven.

P. G. Wodehouse

"TAKE THE WITNESS!"

by Robert Benchley

The late, great Robert Benchley was a man with no malice in him. Unlike some of his humor-writing colleagues, who depend upon barbed commentary and cutting satire for their laughs, Benchley never wrote anything in his humor pieces that might hurt anybody, and even his dramatic criticisms were as gentle and sympathetic as the situation would allow. It isn't surprising that he is one of the most beloved of modern humorists.

To complete the picture, we might add that everything Benchley ever wrote was a minor masterpiece, at least. The selection that follows is, we think, a major one.

NEWSPAPER accounts of trial cross-examinations always bring out the cleverest in me. They induce day dreams in which I am the witness on the stand, and if you don't know some of my imaginary comebacks to an imaginary cross-examiner (Doe vs. Benchley: 482-U.S.-367-398), you have missed some of the most stimulating reading in the history of American jurisprudence.

These little reveries usually take place shortly after I have read the transcript of a trial, while I am on a long taxi ride or seated at a desk with plenty of other work to do. I like them best when I have work to do, as they deplete

me mentally so that I am forced to go and lie down after
a particularly sharp verbal rally. The knowledge that I have
completely floored my adversary, and the imaginary con-
gratulations of my friends (also imaginary), seem more
worth while than any amount of fiddling work done.

During these cross-questionings I am always very calm.
Calm in a nice way, that is—never cocky. However frantic
my inquisitor may wax (and you should see his face at times
—it's purple!), I just sit there, burning him up with each
answer, winning the admiration of the courtroom, and, at
times, even a smile from the judge himself. At the end of
my examination, the judge is crazy about me.

Just what the trial is about, I never get quite clear in my
mind. Sometimes the subject changes in the middle of the
questioning, to allow for the insertion of an especially good
crack on my part. I don't think that I am ever actually the
defendant, although I don't know why I should feel that
I am immune from trial by a jury of my peers—if such
exist.

I am usually testifying in behalf of a friend, or perhaps
as just an impersonal witness for someone whom I do not
know, who, naturally, later becomes my friend for life. It
is Justice that I am after—Justice and a few well-spotted
laughs.

Let us whip right into the middle of my cross-examina-
tion, as I naturally wouldn't want to pull my stuff until I
had been insulted by the lawyer, and you can't really get
insulted simply by having your name and address asked.
I am absolutely fair about these things. If the lawyer will
treat me right, I'll treat him right. He has got to start it. For
a decent cross-examiner, there is no more tractable witness
in the world than I am.

Advancing toward me, with a sneer on his face, he points
a finger at me. (I have sometimes thought of pointing my

finger back at him, but have discarded that as being too
fresh. I don't have to resort to clowning.)

Q—You think you're pretty funny, don't you? *(I have evi-
dently just made some mildly humorous comeback,
nothing smart-alecky, but good enough to make him
look silly.)*
A—I have never given the matter much thought.
Q—Oh, you haven't given the matter much thought, eh?
Well, you seem to be treating this examination as if it
were a minstrel show.
A *(very quietly and nicely)*—I have merely been taking
my cue from your questions. *(You will notice that all
this presupposes quite a barrage of silly questions on his
part, and pat answers on mine, omitted here because I
haven't thought them up. At any rate, it is evident that I
have already got him on the run before this reverie begins.)*
Q—Perhaps you would rather that I conducted this inquiry
in baby talk?
A—If it will make it any easier for you. *(Pandemonium,
which the Court feels that it has to quell, although enjoying it obviously as much as the spectators.)*
Q *(furious)*—I see. Well, here is a question that I think will
be simple enough to elicit an honest answer: Just how
did you happen to know that it was eleven-fifteen when
you saw the defendant?
A—Because I looked at my watch.
Q—And just why did you look at your watch at this par-
ticular time?
A—To see what time it was.
Q—Are you accustomed to looking at your watch often?
A—That is one of the uses to which I often put my watch.
Q—I see. Now, it couldn't, by any chance, have been ten-

fifteen instead of eleven-fifteen when you looked at your watch this time, could it?

A—Yes, sir. It could.

Q—Oh, it *could* have been ten-fifteen?

A—Yes, sir—if I had been in Chicago. (*Not very good, really. I'll work up something better. I move to have that answer stricken from the record.*)

When I feel myself lowering my standards by answering like that, I usually give myself a rest, and, unless something else awfully good pops into my head, I adjourn the court until next day. I can always convene it again when I hit my stride.

If possible, however, I like to drag it out until I have really given my antagonist a big final wallop which practically curls him up on the floor (I may think of one before this goes to press), and, wiping his forehead, he mutters, "Take the witness!"

As I step down from the stand, fresh as a daisy, there is a round of applause which the Court makes no attempt to silence. In fact, I have known certain judges to wink pleasantly at me as I take my seat. Judges are only human, after all.

My only fear is that, if I ever really am called upon to testify in court, I won't be asked the right questions. That *would* be a pretty kettle of fish!

GROUCHO: THE MAN FROM MARX

by Leo Rosten

If you share the enormously popular belief that all dentists are sadists who spend their after-drilling hours thinking up frightening new instruments to put in people's mouths, you're wrong in at least one case—Leo Rosten's. *He* spent his spare time writing, under the pseudonym of Leonard Q. Ross, the now famous *Education of Hyman Kaplan,* which was so successful that he exchanged forever his forceps for a typewriter. Since that time, he has written motion pictures, several serious books on labor and allied topics, and many more excellent humor pieces and books.

We've chosen the following piece for this anthology for two reasons. First of all, it's a good example of the excellent Rosten style of humor. And second of all, we're pushovers for anything about Groucho Marx, our favorite genius.

My HOUSE in California was a sane and sober place until the day the telephone rang and a voice said, "This is Professor Waldemar Strumbelknauff."

"Who?" I asked.

"Let's not quibble," the voice said coldly. "Aren't you ashamed of yourself, beating your children that way? You Cossack. If you were a man you'd come over here and knock

my teeth out. If you were half a man, you'd knock half my
teeth out. I'm sick and tired of your calling up at all hours
of the night to ask for specimens of my nail-clippings."

"Who *is* this?" I fumed.

"It's cads like you who are destroying the American
home. You didn't think I'd take this lying down, did you?
Well, it just happens I *am* lying down. What kind of an
idiot do you take me for—an idiot?"

"Now listen," I raged, "if you—"

"This is the Secretary of the National Committee to Free
Georgia. And I suppose you'll tell me you don't even know
her. A fine kettle of fish. This is Groucho. How *are* you? As
if I really care."

I should, of course, have known it from the first. No one
else could have delivered so brazen and bewildering a
monologue, in so coldly indignant a voice, with such a mix-
ture of defiance and lunacy.

My life was never the same after Groucho Marx learned
my phone number. At one time or another, I have been
telephoned by a barnacle-scraper named Formosa Greulen-
heimer, by the president of the Society for Counterfeit
Money, by Captain Raoul P. Clamhead of the Iranian FBI.
I have been awakened at ungodly hours to be asked
whether I wanted my wife replaced, my lawn re-seeded,
or my children sold.

I have been identified to strangers as the brain behind
J. P. Morgan, the man who invented the deep-freeze, a
tapioca-runner from Acapulco, and the manager of that
celebrated Moscow movie house, Loew's Kremlin. My wife
has been tipped off to the fact that originally I had two
heads; my editors have been warned that I write under the
pseudonym G. B. Shaw; my eleven-year-old son has been
accused of being a midget who graduated from Yale in

1908, whom I keep undersized by the injection of antigland juices. It hasn't been an easy life.

One night, when I was riding in a car with this creature from the moon, I suddenly remembered that it was my father's birthday. "Stop at a Western Union office," I said. "I want to wire my father." "What's the matter?" asked Groucho. "Can't he stand up by himself?"

A few months later, when Groucho returned to California from a trip into Mexico, the customs officer asked him, "What's your name?"

"Marx."

"Birthplace?"

"New York."

"Occupation?"

"Smuggler."

Trying to carry on a conversation with the man gives you the feeling that you've fallen into a Bendix with Betty Hutton. You get dead-panned, misunderstood, challenged, misquoted, and—in the end—routed by whatever wild notion fits into that demoniacal mind.

His way with those who believe in reason is devastating. In the middle of a political discussion, he is liable to rise gravely and announce, "Gentlemen, they have fired on Fort Sumter." After the last election, on the day Dewey broke off diplomatic relations with Gallup, Marx issued the following statement: "The only way a Republican is going to get into the White House is by marrying Margaret."

Shortly after *that*, on his Christmas radio program, he asked a seven-year-old if there were any questions she would like to ask Santa Claus. "Yes," said the child, "I would like to know how he can get all over the world in one night." "Well, Dewey got all over being President in one night," said Groucho.

To ask him a direct question is to put your sanity in his hands. A fan once accosted him on the street, pestering him with adulation, until Groucho said, "I never forget a face—but in your case I'll be glad to make an exception." To an actress who tried to flatter him by cooing, "You're a man after my own heart," he leered, "That's not all I'm after."

To another actress, who consulted him about a career in the theater, he said, "My advice to you and to all struggling actresses is this: keep struggling. If you keep struggling, you won't get into trouble. And if you don't get into trouble, you'll never be much of an actress." If you're around him during one of these moods, you feel like the bird who flew too low and got caught in a badminton game.

Many public-spirited citizens have tried to stump him. During all the years the four Marx Brothers were the darlings of Broadway, Chico, no slouch as a zany himself, tried to throw Groucho off-balance. In a show mysteriously called *I'll Say She Is,* Chico was in the wings watching the scene in which Groucho, as Napoleon, was making demented love to Josephine. Chico decided to step on stage suddenly, announcing, "Emperor, the garbage man is here!" His triumphant grin was erased when Groucho replied, "Tell him we don't want any." Later, trumpets sounded in the distance playing the *Marseillaise.* Groucho rose solemnly. "Our national anthem—the Mayonnaise. Ah, well, the army must be dressing." In *Horsefeathers,* a play for young and old, a foolhardy actor broke into Groucho's office to declaim, "Jennings has been waiting for an hour and is waxing wroth!" "Tell Roth to wax Jennings for a change," said the master idly.

The soundest advice I can give people, for their own protection, is never to say *anything* to the man. Whenever I am near him, I fall into a precautionary trance. At a baseball game I attended one night as his guest, at the home grounds of the Hollywood Stars, his comments were so confusing that I did not know whether I was watching the Stars, seeing them, or had been taken in a strait jacket to a grudge match between some men from Mars. To a batter who poked feebly at a high one, Marx yelled: "You haven't enough strength to beat your wife." A second baseman incurred his wrath by striking out, popping up, and striking out again. In the ninth inning, this unfortunate soul managed to hit a double. As the crowd cheered, Groucho said bitterly, "That's the first time in his life that guy's been on second without a glove."

During a charity match between a team of Comedians and a team of Actors, Groucho was elected manager of the Comedians. As Jack Benny, the lead-off man, went to the plate, Groucho said, "All right, Benny, get up there and hit a home run." Mr. Benny struck out. Mr. Marx promptly resigned. "I can't manage a team that won't follow instructions."

Nor is it any safer to accompany him to a prize fight. Any well-informed man knows, of course, that the Marx Brothers, possessed of a wild impulse one night, signed up a heavyweight whom they dubbed Canvasback Cohen. According to experts, the art of manly defense has never recovered from that calamitous partnership. No one ever knew *what* Groucho was liable to advise his gladiator. It is said that between rounds of one fight, he examined his mutilated protégé, turned to the audience, and called, "Is there a doctor in the house?" A kindly man in the fourth row rose. "I'm a doctor." Groucho waved, "How are you enjoying the fight, Doc?" They also say the episode occurred in a Marx Brothers play, when Groucho interrupted a scene by stepping to the footlights to inquire, "Is there a doctor in the house?" When a doctor rose, Groucho said,

"If you're a doctor, why aren't you at the hospital making your patients miserable, instead of wasting your time here with that blonde?"

I must also warn readers against attending weddings, wakes or wars with the man. During the last war, when he went overseas for USO to demoralize our troops, he was in the headquarters of a general when the Signal Corps phone rang. Groucho picked up the instrument and crooned, "World War Two-oo."

Any formal occasion, any organized ritual or celebration is meat for the man's dementia. Some years ago, he was taken to a seance with some Hollywood natives who had become entranced by the supernatural powers of a spiritualist then enjoying high esteem in the movie colony. The medium, a woman of baffling talents, produced voices from the beyond, conjured up ancient spirits, conversed in Comanche with an Indian princess, and served as a remarkably efficient intermediary between those who were here and those who were hereafter. It might still be regarded as the most convincing demonstration of occult power ever witnessed, had not the medium, flushed with success, asked, "Are there any more questions?" Mr. Marx had a question: "What's the capital of South Dakota?"

Two years ago, the delinquent mind of Groucho Marx was drafted into the service of ABC for a quiz-show conceived by a producer named John Guedel and entitled *You Bet Your Life*. When I heard this, my heart sank. (I did not tell him that my heart sank; I was afraid he would reply, "Sank you.") Wise men in the world of radio had long maintained that the Marx humor was a very special brand, cherished by a small and fanatical band, but much too rare and satirical to win favor from mass audiences.

Groucho was to interview three pairs of contestants informally, before asking the usual questions and distributing the usual moola. It was hoped that his inhuman capacity for ad libs might brighten up the body of a routine which, in other versions on the air, was beginning to suffer from acute hardening of the arteries. The night the program opened, it is said, ABC's top officials sat in a circle and kept their fingers crossed.

Well, within a short year, Marx won the Peabody Award (radio's equivalent of the Pulitzer Prize) and created an art-form which inspired one critic to rave, "He is a fresh breeze blowing through the stale gags of radio." This accomplished, he moved over to the 9 p.m. Wednesday spot on CBS, shot to seventh place in the national Hooper ratings, and accepted a subsidy from De Soto and Plymouth. Subsequently, he went on to equal success in television.

On the air, Groucho is unlike any other comedian. He does not tell stories. He does not tell jokes. He does not use contrived "situations." He does not follow a script. He does not present guest stars. He does not employ straight-men, bit players, or stooges. He does not swap banter with the orchestra. He does nothing, in fact, except chat with his contestants, and about the most mundane matters: "Are you married?" "Have you any children?" "How did you meet your wife?" "How many banks have you broken into lately?" and so on. The reason you hear such strange, loud noises from the audience (sounds known in the trade as boffs, yaks and boffolas) is that his disarming questions lead to complications of an unearthly and deranged character. I can only try to reproduce the flavor from a dazed and no doubt unreliable memory:

GROUCHO: Are you married?
MAN: Well . . . yes and no.
GROUCHO: Good for you! That's the way to be. What do you mean, yes and no?

MAN: I mean I'm going to marry the same woman I was once married to.

GROUCHO: Didn't it *take* the first time?

MAN: Well, I guess not.

GROUCHO: No guessing, please. Not on this quiz show. Tell me, Fallen Arches, how did you meet your wife?

MAN: We were kids together.

GROUCHO: Well, that's possible—but how did you meet her?

MAN: You see I drive a truck—

GROUCHO: You ran over her?

MAN: No, she was in the barn—

GROUCHO: You drove the truck into a barn?

MAN: *No.* You see, she was a farmer's daughter, and they had been missing their chickens—

GROUCHO: They were lonely for chickens?

MAN: No, they had been *missing* them, so they turned a light on in the barnyard, and one night I drove up to get some turkeys, and her father said the turkeys were in the barn—

GROUCHO: You married a *turkey?*

MAN: No, no. As I went to the barn, a skunk started for the chicken house—and she yelled, "Get that skunk."

GROUCHO: A fine way for her to talk about her future husband.

MAN: —and I jumped on the skunk, and she fell on the skunk, too, and we started going out together, because no one else would go out with either of us.

On one program, when a contestant developed mike-fright, unable to utter a word, Groucho said, "Either this man is dead or my watch has stopped."

When a member of the House of Representatives said

he earned his living in Congress, Groucho asked, "How long have you been incongruous?" When a schoolteacher confessed she was "approaching 40," the master queried, "From which direction?"

To a Chinese contestant who said he was 24, Groucho asked, "In years or in yen?" When the boy said you don't count age in yen, our man replied, "Oh, no? I have a yen to be 21 again."

His puns are little short of criminal. Mention the Alps, and he will say, "Ah, the Alps. I love the Alps. So does God, because God alps them that alp themselves." Talk about big-game hunting, and he is likely to go off on a monologue such as the one he made famous in *Animal Crackers*. "Once I went big-game hunting in Africa. What an active life we led! Up at 6, breakfast at 6:15, back in bed by 6:30. One day I shot an elephant in my pajamas. How he got into my pajamas, I'll never know. It was hard to get his tusks off. In Alabama, the Tuscaloosa."

Tell him, as one fan did, "It's certainly a pleasure to meet Groucho Marx," and he will sneer, "*I've* known him for years, and I can tell you it's no pleasure." To the Friars Club in Hollywood, from which he recently resigned, he sent the following note: "I do not care to belong to a club that accepts people like me as members."

The antic universe in which the man lives can further be illustrated by the following excerpts from his radio asylum:

GROUCHO: How did you get your husband?
NURSE: I haven't any husband.
GROUCHO: Are you married?
NURSE: No.
GROUCHO: Well, that explains it, I suppose.

GROUCHO: So you came here from Australia. How **did** you get to the United States?

GIRL: I flew over, by plane.

GROUCHO: A girl would be a fool to try it any other way.

GROUCHO: Is it true that you wrestlers fake most of your matches?

PROFESSIONAL WRESTLER: That's a dirty rumor!

GROUCHO: How many dirty rumors have you wrestled lately?

The radio show on which this humor is committed each week, to the delight of more than twelve million listeners, is the apple of Groucho's eye. He recently asked David Miller, the movie director, "Did you hear my show last night?" "Only the first ten minutes," said Miller. "The studio called me away." "A fine friend *you've* turned out to be," said Groucho. "*I* listened to the whole program from start to finish. That's the kind of friend *I* am."

Being a friend of his isn't something you do lightly. You have to be in perfect physical condition. During the darkest days of rationing, Oscar Levant flew into Los Angeles from a grueling concert tour. In a burst of camaraderie, Groucho said, "Oscar, you look tired. Why don't you come to my house for dinner? I've got the most wonderful cook in town, I've saved a steak four inches thick, and we'll have a dessert that's out of this world." Levant sighed gratefully, "What's your address?" "Wouldn't *you* like to know?" asked Groucho, and walked away.

Earl Wilson's celebrated BW was once rash enough to make conversation by venturing, "I made a stew last night for dinner." "Anyone I know?" asked Groucho.

When writer S. J. Perelman, a man of comparable talent in the *non sequitur* trade, was being given a testimonial dinner in Beverly Hills, Groucho introduced the guest of honor in these touching words: "Here is a man who has not let success go to his head—a man who is humble and unspoiled. He is as unassuming, as comfortable to be with as an old glove—and just about as interesting."

In person, Mr. Marx has a wall-eyed stare, the lope of an arthritic roue, and a moustache which he claims belongs to his maid. His leer, the most distinguished characteristic of an otherwise innocent face, suggests a wolf who is alarmingly intimate with evil. His voice—the flattest, most bored monotone in the business—resembles that of a sardonic owl. For all I know, he may *be* an owl.

His wit, which he delivers with an expression of fine disgust, is a form of surrealism which has made him the pet of intellectuals, logicians and schizophrenics. An Einstein of irrelevance, his unhinged reasoning is a good example of what Bertrand Russell calls "the set paradox," and what others call logical lunacy. His thinking processes (if that is what you can call his rides on a mental roller coaster) resemble those of the German philosopher who dreamed about a knife without a blade which had no handle.

In closing, I must confess that I undertook this article with a good deal of uneasiness. I knew that while writing it I would be overcome by the feeling that I was haunted. I especially feared that after Mr. Marx had read what I have written—oh, Lord, my telephone is ringing!

Dear Mr. Rosten:

My spies report that you are preparing a piece about me
for that excellent journal, LOOK. I am greatly flattered,
since I have subscribed to LOOK for the past thirty years.
I can't understand this, because LOOK hasn't been published
that long. Besides, I can't read.

Scandal-mongers will no doubt give you a mass of
malicious gossip concerning an escapade in Greenwich, Connecticut, when the manager of a local theatre wouldn't let me smoke
my cigar. My brothers and I refused to go on. The manager
confiscated our trunks. We confiscated the manager—and set
fire to the theatre. This is all a dirty lie, and if you
print it, I'll sue to the hilt. It wasn't Greenwich; it was
Bridgeport.

To keep the record straight (which won't do you any
good unless you have a 35 RPM straight-record player), I give
you the following inside dope:

My brother Harpo is not really a deaf-mute; he just
can't think of anything to say...My moustache is genuine;
it belongs to my maid...Add a dash of ammonia when cleaning
your stove, and the grease will disappear; then light a
match, and the roof will disappear...The four Marx brothers
are not really brothers; they're sisters...Ohio won the Rose
Bowl game 17-14...

This information is, of course, somewhat scatterbrained.
Hoping you are the same, I am

Groucho

Groucho

Leo Rosten's story on Groucho Marx appeared originally in
Look Magazine. The above letter reached Rosten while he was
working on the article, and is reproduced through the kind permission of Mr. Rosten, *Look* Magazine, and Professor Waldemar
Strumbelknauff.

SOMEWHERE A ROSCOE . . .

by S. J. Perelman

Have you ever been reading a mystery story of the hard-boiled private eye school, noticed that the gunshots and wisecracks seemed to turn up in curiously familiar and expected spots in the story, and begun to wonder if you've read the yarn somewhere before? The chances, as S. J. Perelman points out in the next selection, are that you have, though in slightly different form and under a different title.

Here is "Somewhere a Roscoe . . . ," S. J. Perleman's penetrating and hilarious analysis of the curious structural similarities in one series of private eye adventures.

THIS IS the story of a mind that found itself. About two years ago I was moody, discontented, restless, almost a character in a Russian novel. I used to lie on my bed for days drinking tea out of a glass (I was one of the first in this country to drink tea out of a glass; at that time fashionable people drank from their cupped hands). Underneath, I was still a lively, fun-loving American boy who liked nothing better than to fish with a bent pin. In short, I had become a remarkable combination of Raskolnikov and Mark Tidd.

One day I realized how introspective I had grown and

decided to talk to myself like a Dutch uncle. "Luik here, Mynheer," I began (I won't give you the accent, but honestly it was a riot), "you've overtrained. You're stale. Open up a few new vistas—go out and get some fresh air!" Well, I bustled about, threw some things into a bag—orange peels, apple cores and the like—and went out for a walk. A few minutes later I picked up from a park bench a tattered pulp magazine called *Spicy Detective. . . .* Talk about your turning points!

I hope nobody minds my making love in public, but if Culture Publications, Inc., of 900 Market Street, Wilmington, Delaware, will have me, I'd like to marry them. Yes, I know—call it a school-boy crush, puppy love, the senseless infatuation of a callow youth for a middle-aged, worldly-wise publishing house; I still don't care. I love them because they are the publishers of not only *Spicy Detective* but also *Spicy Western, Spicy Mystery* and *Spicy Adventure.* And I love them most because their prose is so soft and warm.

"Arms and the man I sing," sang Vergil some twenty centuries ago, preparing to celebrate the wanderings of Aeneas. If ever a motto was tailormade for the masthead of Culture Publications, Inc., it is "Arms and the Woman," for in *Spicy Detective* they have achieved the sauciest blend of libido and murder this side of Gilles de Rais. They have juxtaposed the steely automatic and the frilly pantie and found that it pays off. Above all, they have given the world Dan Turner, the apotheosis of all private detectives. Out of Ma Barker by Dashiell Hammett's Sam Spade, let him characterize himself in the opening paragraph of "Corpse in the Closet," from the July, 1937, issue:

> I opened my bedroom closet. A half-dressed feminine corpse sagged into my arms. . . . It's a damned screwy feeling to reach for pajamas and find a cadaver instead.

Mr. Turner, you will perceive, is a man of sentiment, and it occasionally gets him into a tight corner. For example, in "Killer's Harvest" (July, 1938) he is retained to escort a young matron home from the Cocoanut Grove in Los Angeles:

Zarah Trenwick was a wow in a gown of silver lamé that stuck to her lush curves like a coating of varnish. Her makeup was perfect; her strapless dress displayed plenty of evidence that she still owned a cargo of lure. Her bare shoulders were snowy, dimpled. The upper slopes of her breast were squeezed upward and partly overflowed the tight bodice, like whipped cream.

To put it mildly, Dan cannot resist the appeal of a pretty foot, and disposing of Zarah's drunken husband ("I clipped him on the button. His hip pockets bounced on the floor"), he takes this charlotte russe to her apartment. Alone with her, the policeman in him succumbs to the man, and "she fed me a kiss that throbbed all the way down my fallen arches," when suddenly:

From the doorway a roscoe said "Kachow!" and a slug creased the side of my noggin. Neon lights exploded inside my think-tank . . . She was as dead as a stuffed mongoose . . . I wasn't badly hurt. But I don't like to be shot at. I don't like dames to be rubbed out when I'm flinging woo at them.

With an irritable shrug, Dan phones the homicide detail and reports Zarah's passing in this tender obituary: "Zarah Trenwick just got blasted to hellangone in her tepee at the Gayboy. Drag your underwear over here—and bring a meat-wagon." Then he goes in search of the offender:

I drove over to Argyle; parked in front of Fane Trenwick's modest stash . . . I thumbed the bell. The door opened. A Chink house-boy gave me the slant-eyed focus. "Missa Tlenwick, him sleep. You go way, come tomollow. Too late fo'

vlisito'." I said "Nerts to you, Confucius," and gave him a shove
on the beezer.

Zarah's husband, wrenched out of bed without the silly
formality of a search warrant, establishes an alibi depend-
ing upon one Nadine Wendell. In a trice Dan crosses the
city and makes his gentle way into the lady's boudoir, only
to discover again what a frail vessel he is *au fond:*

The fragrant scent of her red hair tickled my smeller; the
warmth of her slim young form set fire to my arterial system.
After all, I'm as human as the next gazabo.

The next gazabo must be all too human, because Dan
betrays first Nadine and then her secret; namely, that she
pistolled Zarah Trenwick for reasons too numerous to mention. If you feel you must know them, they appear on page
110, cheek by jowl with some fascinating advertisements
for loaded dice and wealthy sweethearts, either of which
will be sent you in plain wrapper if you'll forward a dollar
to the Majestic Novelty Company of Janesville, Wisconsin.

The deeper one goes into the Dan Turner saga, the more
one is struck by the similarity between the case confront-
ing Dan in the current issue and those in the past. The
murders follow an exact, rigid pattern almost like the ritual
of a bullfight or a classic Chinese play. Take "Veiled Lady,"
in the October, 1937, number of *Spicy Detective.* Dan is
flinging some woo at a Mrs. Brantham in her apartment at
the exclusive Gayboy Arms, which apparently excludes
everybody but assassins:

From behind me a roscoe belched "Chow-chow!" A pair of
slugs buzzed past my left ear, almost nicked my cranium. Mrs.
Brantham sagged back against the pillow of the lounge . . .
She was as dead as an iced catfish.

Or this vignette from "Falling Star," out of the Septem-
ber, 1936, issue:

The roscoe said "Chow!" and spat a streak of flame past my shoulder . . . The Filipino cutie was lying where I'd last seen her. She was as dead as a smoked herring.

And again, from "Dark Star of Death," January, 1938:

From a bedroom a roscoe said: "Whr-r-rang!" and a lead pill split the ozone past my noggin . . . Kane Fewster was on the floor. There was a bullet hole through his think-tank. He was as dead as a fried oyster.

And still again, from "Brunette Bump-off," May, 1938:

And then, from an open window beyond the bed, a roscoe coughed "Ka-chow!" . . . I said, "What the hell—!" and hit the floor with my smeller . . . A brunette jane was lying there, half out of the mussed covers. . . . She was as dead as vaudeville.

The next phase in each of these dramas follows with all the cold beauty and inevitability of a legal brief. The roscoe has hardly spoken, coughed, or belched before Dan is off through the canebrake, his nostrils filled with the heavy scent of Nuit de Noël. Somewhere, in some dimly lit boudoir, waits a voluptuous parcel of womanhood who knows all about the horrid deed. Even if she doesn't Dan makes a routine check anyway. The premises are invariably guarded by an Oriental whom Dan is obliged to expunge. Compare the scene at Fane Trenwick's modest stash with this one from "Find That Corpse" (November, 1937):

A sleepy Chink maid in pajamas answered my ring. She was a cute little slant-eyed number. I said "Is Mr. Polznak home?" She shook her head. "Him up on location in Flesno. Been gone two week." I said "Thanks. I'll have a gander for myself." I pushed past her. She started to yip . . . "Shut up!" I growled. She kept on trying to make a noise. So I popped her on the button. She dropped.

It is a fairly safe bet that Mr. Polznak has forgotten the adage that a watched pot never boils and has left behind a dewy-eyed coryphée clad in the minimum of chiffon demanded by the postal authorities. The poet in Dan ineluctably vanquishes the flatfoot ("Dark Star of Death"): "I glued my glims on her blond loveliness; couldn't help myself. The covers had skidded down from her gorgeous, dimpled shoulders; I could see plenty of delishful, she-male epidermis." The trumpets blare again; some expert capework by our *torero*, and "Brunette Bump-off": "Then she fed me a kiss that sent a charge of steam past my gozzle . . . Well, I'm as human as the next gink."

From then on, the author's typewriter keys infallibly fuse in a lump of hot metal and it's all over but the shouting of the culprit and *"Look, Men: One Hundred Breezy Fotos!"* Back in his stash, his roscoe safely within reach, Dan Turner lays his weary noggin on a pillow, resting up for the November issue. And unless you're going to need me for something this afternoon, I intend to do the same. I'm *bushed.*

FATHER WAKES UP THE VILLAGE

by Clarence Day

Let's face it: Clarence Day's father liked ice, plenty of ice, and when he liked and wanted something, he was blasted if he was going to have to do without it. The selection that follows—the story of how Father went into action when the iceman missed a delivery—is one of the funniest in the *Life with Father* series.

Clarence Day began to write when a sudden and crippling attack of arthritis turned him into a permanent invalid. His stories and books were immediate successes, and the play based on his *Life with Father* series enjoyed one of the longest runs in Broadway history.

ONE OF the most disgraceful features of life in the country, Father often declared, was the general inefficiency and slackness of small village tradesmen. He said he had originally supposed that such men were interested in business, and that that was why they had opened their shops and sunk capital in them, but no, they never used them for anything but gossip and sleep. They took no interest in civilized ways. Hadn't heard of them, probably. He said that of course if he were camping out on the veldt or the tundra, he would expect few conveniences in the neighborhood and would do his best to forego them, but why should he be confronted with the wilds twenty miles from New York?

Usually, when Father talked this way, he was thinking of ice. He strongly objected to spending even one day of his life without a glass of cold water beside his plate at every meal. There was never any difficulty about this in our home in the city. A great silver ice-water pitcher stood on the sideboard all day, and when Father was home its outer surface was frosted with cold. When he had gone to the office, the ice was allowed to melt sometimes, and the water got warmish, but never in the evening, or on Sundays, when Father might want some. He said he liked water, he told us it was one of Nature's best gifts, but he said that like all her gifts it was unfit for human consumption unless served in a suitable manner. And the only right way to serve water was icy cold.

It was still more important that each kind of wine should be served at whatever the right temperature was for it. And kept at it, too. No civilized man would take dinner without wine, Father said, and no man who knew the first thing about it would keep his wine in hot cellars. Mother thought this was a mere whim of Father's. She said he was fussy. How about people who lived in apartments, she asked him, who didn't have cellars? Father replied that civilized persons didn't live in apartments.

One of the first summers that Father ever spent in the country, he rented a furnished house in Irvington on the Hudson, not far from New York. It had a garden, a stable, and one or two acres of woods, and Father arranged to camp out there with many misgivings. He took a train for New York every morning at eight-ten, after breakfast, and he got back between five and six, bringing anything special we might need along with him, such as a basket of peaches from the city, or a fresh package of his own private coffee.

Things went well until one day in August the ice-man didn't come. It was hot, he and his horses were tired, and he hated to come to us anyhow because the house we had rented was perched up on top of a hill. He said afterward that on this particular day he had not liked the idea of making his horses drag the big ice-wagon up that sharp and steep road to sell us fifty cents' worth of ice. Besides, all his ice was gone anyhow—the heat had melted it on him. He had four or five other good reasons. So he didn't come.

Father was in town. The rest of us waited in astonishment, wondering what could be the matter. We were so used to the regularity and punctilio of life in the city that it seemed unbelievable to us that the ice-man would fail to appear. We discussed it at lunch. Mother said that the minute he arrived she would have to give him a talking to. After lunch had been over an hour and he still hadn't come, she got so worried about what Father would say that she decided to send to the village.

There was no telephone, of course. There were no motors. She would have liked to spare the horse if she could, for he had been worked hard that week. But as this was a crisis, she sent for Morgan, the coachman, and told him to bring up the dog-cart.

The big English dog-cart arrived. Two of us boys and the coachman drove off. The sun beat down on our heads. Where the heavy harness was rubbing on Brownie's coat, he broke out into a thick, whitish lather. Morgan was sullen. When we boys were along he couldn't take off his stiff black high hat or unbutton his thick, padded coat. Worse still, from his point of view, he couldn't stop at a bar for a drink. That was why Mother had sent us along with him, of course, and he knew it.

We arrived at the little town after a while and I went into the Coal & Ice Office. A wiry-looking old clerk was dozing in a corner, his chair tilted back and his chin resting on his dingy shirt-front. I woke this clerk up. I told him about the crisis at our house.

He listened unwillingly, and when I had finished he said it was a very hot day.

I waited. He spat. He said he didn't see what he could do, because the ice-house was locked.

I explained earnestly that this was the Day family and that something must be done right away.

He hunted around his desk a few minutes, found his chewing tobacco, and said, "Well, sonny, I'll see what I can do about it."

I thanked him very much, as that seemed to me to settle the matter. I went back to the dog-cart. Brownie s check-rein had been unhooked, and he stood with his head hanging down. He looked sloppy. It wouldn't have been so bad with a buggy, but a slumpy horse in a dog-cart can look pretty awful. Also, Morgan was gone. He reappeared soon, coming out of a side door down the street, buttoning up his coat, but with his hat tilted back. He looked worse than the horse.

We checked up the weary animal's head again and drove slowly home. A hot little breeze in our rear moved our dust along with us. At the foot of the hill, we boys got out, to spare Brownie our extra weight. We unhooked his check-rein again. He dragged the heavy cart up.

Mother was sitting out on the piazza. I said the ice would come soon now. We waited.

It was a long afternoon.

At five o'clock, Brownie was hitched up again. The coach-man and I drove back to the village. We had to meet Father's train. We also had to break the bad news to him that he would have no ice-water for dinner, and that there didn't seem to be any way to chill his Rhine wine.

The village was as sleepy as ever, but when Father arrived and learned what the situation was, he said it would have to wake up. He told me that he had had a long, trying day at the office, the city was hotter than the Desert of Sahara, and he was completely worn out, but that if any ice-man imagined for a moment he could behave in that manner, he, Father, would take his damned head off. He strode into the Coal & Ice Office.

When he came out, he had the clerk with him, and the clerk had put on his hat and was vainly trying to calm Father down. He was promising that he himself would come with the ice-wagon if the driver had left, and deliver all the ice we could use, and he'd be there inside an hour.

Father said, "Inside of an hour be hanged, you'll have to come quicker than that."

The clerk got rebellious. He pointed out that he'd have to go to the stables and hitch up the horses himself, and then get someone to help him hoist a block of ice out of the ice-house. He said it was 'most time for his supper and he wasn't used to such work. He was only doing it as a favor to Father. He was just being neighborly.

Father said he'd have to be neighborly in a hurry, because he wouldn't stand it, and he didn't know what the devil the ice company meant by such actions.

The clerk said it wasn't his fault, was it? It was the driver's.

This was poor tactics, of course, because it wound Father up again. He wasn't interested in whose fault it was, he said. It was everybody's. What he wanted was ice and plenty of it, and he wanted it in time for his dinner. A small crowd which had collected by this time listened admiringly as Father shook his finger at the clerk and said he dined at six-thirty.

The clerk went loping off toward the stables to hitch up the big horses. Father waited till he'd turned the corner.

Followed by the crowd, Father marched to the butcher's.

After nearly a quarter of an hour, the butcher and his assistant came out, unwillingly carrying what seemed to be a coffin, wrapped in a black mackintosh. It was a huge cake of ice.

Father got in, in front, sat on the box seat beside me, and took up the reins. We drove off. The coachman was on the rear seat, sitting back-to-back to us, keeping the ice from sliding out with the calves of his legs. Father went a few doors up the street to a little house-furnishings shop and got out again.

I went in the shop with him this time. I didn't want to miss any further scenes of this performance. Father began proceedings by demanding to see all the man's ice-boxes. There were only a few. Father selected the largest he had. Then, when the sale seemed arranged, and when the proprietor was smiling broadly with pleasure at this sudden windfall, Father said he was buying that refrigerator only on two conditions.

The first was that it had to be delivered at his home before dinner. Yes, now. Right away. The shopkeeper explained over and over that this was impossible, but that he'd have it up the next morning, sure. Father said no, he didn't want it the next morning, he had to have it at once. He added that he dined at six-thirty, and that there was no time to waste.

The shopkeeper gave in.

The second condition, which was then put to him firmly, was staggering. Father announced that that ice-box must be delivered to him full of ice.

The man said he was not in the ice business.

Father said, "Very well then. I don't want it."

The man said obstinately that it was an excellent ice-box.

Father made a short speech. It was the one that we had heard so often at home about the slackness of village tradesmen, and he put such strong emotion and scorn in it that his voice rang through the shop. He closed it by saying, "An ice-box is of no use to a man without ice, and if you haven't the enterprise, the gumption, to sell your damned goods to a customer who wants them delivered in condition to use, you had better shut up your shop and be done with it. Not in the ice business, hey? You aren't in business at all!" He strode out.

The dealer came to the door just as Father was getting into the dog-cart, and called out anxiously, "All right, Mr. Day. I'll get that refrigerator filled for you and send it up right away."

Father drove quickly home. A thunderstorm seemed to be brewing and this had waked Brownie up, or else Father was putting some of his own supply of energy into him. The poor old boy probably needed it as again he climbed the steep hill. I got out at the foot, and as I walked along behind I saw that Morgan was looking kind of desperate, trying to sit in the correct position with his arms folded while he held in the ice with his legs. The big cake was continually slipping and sliding around under the seat and doing its best to plunge out. It had bumped against his calves all the way home. They must have got good and cold.

When the dog-cart drew up at our door, Father remained seated a moment while Morgan, the waitress, and I pulled and pushed at the ice. The mackintosh had come off it by this time. We dumped it out on the grass. A little later, after Morgan had unharnessed and hurriedly rubbed down the horse, he ran back to help us boys break the cake up, push the chunks around to the back door, and cram them into the ice-box while Father was dressing for dinner.

Mother had calmed down by this time. The Rhine wine was cooling. "Don't get it too cold," Father called.

Then the ice-man arrived.

The old clerk was with him, like a warden in charge of

a prisoner. Mother stepped out to meet them, and at once gave the ice-man the scolding that had been waiting for him all day.

The clerk asked how much ice we wanted. Mother said we didn't want any now. Mr. Day had brought home some, and we had no room for more in the ice-box.

The ice-man looked at the clerk. The clerk tried to speak, but no words came.

Father put his head out of the window. "Take a hundred pounds, Vinnie," he said. "There's another box coming."

A hundred-pound block was brought into the house and heaved into the washtub. The waitress put the mackintosh over it. The ice-wagon left.

Just as we all sat down to dinner, the new ice-box arrived, full.

Mother was provoked. She said "Really, Clare!" crossly. "Now what am I to do with that piece that's waiting out in the washtub?"

Father chuckled.

She told him he didn't know the first thing about keeping house, and went out to the laundry with the waitress to tackle the problem. The thunderstorm broke and crashed. We boys ran around shutting the windows upstairs.

Father's soul was at peace. He dined well, and he had his coffee and cognac served to him on the piazza. The storm was over by then. Father snuffed a deep breath of the sweet-smelling air and smoked his evening cigar.

"Clarence," he said, "King Solomon had the right idea about these things. 'Whatsoever thy hand findeth to do,' Solomon said, 'do thy damnedest.'"

Mother called me inside. "Whose mackintosh is that?" she asked anxiously. "Katie's torn a hole in the back."

I heard Father saying contentedly on the piazza, "I like plenty of ice."

SONG TO BE SUNG BY THE FATHER OF INFANT FEMALE CHILDREN

by Ogden Nash

My heart leaps up when I behold
A rainbow in the sky;
Contrariwise, my blood runs cold
When little boys go by.
For little boys as little boys,
No special hate I carry,
But now and then they grow to men,
And when they do, they marry.
No matter how they tarry,
Eventually they marry.
And, swine among the pearls,
They marry little girls.

Oh, somewhere, somewhere, an infant plays,
With parents who feed and clothe him.
Their lips are sticky with pride and praise,
But I have begun to loathe him.
Yes, I loathe with a loathing shameless
This child who to me is nameless.
This bachelor child in his carriage
Gives never a thought to marriage,

But a person can hardly say knife
Before he will hunt him a wife.

I never see an infant (male),
A-sleeping in the sun,
Without I turn a trifle pale
And think, is *he* the one?
Oh, first he'll want to crop his curls,
And then he'll want a pony,
And then he'll think of pretty girls
And holy matrimony.
He'll put away his pony,
And sigh for matrimony.
A cat without a mouse
Is he without a spouse.

Oh, somewhere he bubbles bubbles of milk,
And quietly sucks his thumbs.
His cheeks are roses painted on silk,
And his teeth are tucked in his gums.
But alas, the teeth will begin to grow,
And the bubbles will cease to bubble;
Given a score of years or so,
The roses will turn to stubble.
He'll sell a bond, or he'll write a book,
And his eyes will get that acquisitive look,
And raging and ravenous for the kill,
He'll boldly ask for the hand of Jill.
This infant whose middle
Is diapered still
Will want to marry
My daughter Jill.

Oh sweet be his slumber and moist his middle!
My dreams, I fear, are infanticiddle.
A fig for embryo Lohengrins!
I'll open all of his safety pins,
I'll pepper his powder, and salt his bottle,
And give him readings from Aristotle.
Sand for his spinach I'll gladly bring,
And Tabasco sauce for his teething ring,
And an elegant, elegant alligator
To play with in his perambulator.
Then perhaps he'll struggle through fire and water
To marry somebody else's daughter.

CAPSULE CRITICISM

by Alexander Woollcott

In their recent encyclopedic volume about the theatrical world, *Show Biz,* coauthors Abel Green and Joe Laurie, Jr., discuss tricky producers who note, for example, the line, "It took magnificent gall to bring this play to Broadway," in the *New York Times* review, and promptly head their ads for the show, "'. . . Magnificent . . .' says the *Times*."

It's doubtful, however, if the producers of the shows discussed in the next selection ever did anything of the sort; in all likelihood, they were too feeble and broken to do anything except apply ice packs to the head and groan. "Capsule Criticism," as you've probably gathered, is a collection of the masterpieces among unfavorable reviews—the prize comments of the most famous of the tearers-down.

Alexander Woollcott, who wrote "Capsule Criticism," was a curious paradox—a man whose radio talks and magazine articles and books often dripped with saccharine good cheer and sentimentality, and who personally was famous and feared for his vitriolic wit. For a fuller picture of Woollcott, and for some examples of his own capsule criticisms of people around him, see the selection from *The Man Who Came to Dinner* in this anthology.

THERE IS a popular notion that a dramatic criticism, to be worthy of the name, must be an article of at least one

thousand words, mostly polysyllables and all devoted—
perfectly devoted—to the grave discussion of some play as
written and performed. To this notion, it must be sadly
admitted, each generation of writers on the theater have
lent some color.

In such an article it is presumed that there will be one
judicious use of the word "adequate" and one resort to the
expression "treading the boards"; also at least one regret-
ful shaking of the head over the hopeless inferiority of the
performance in question to (a) the way it was done in some
other country two years before or (b) the way it would
have been done in the critic's own country thirty years ago.
Such ingredients are expected with reasonable confidence.
But one thing is certain. The piece, to be real dramatic criticism, can scarcely be briefer than a thousand words.

The tradition of prolixity and the dullness in all such
writing is as old as Aristotle and as lasting as William
Archer. A man who will talk gaily of a play will yet feel a
certain solemnity wetting down his spirits the moment he
finds himself called upon to discuss it in print. Even Mr.
Dickens, who could take his beloved theater lightly enough
when he was weaving it into a novel and who always
packed his letters full of the most engaging accounts of the
farces and melodramas he was seeing, became rigid with
self-importance and chill with scrupulosity the moment he
knew he was reviewing a piece for publication. If he had
undertaken to supply such comment to "The Examiner" or
to our own "Atlantic," a voice within him seemed to whisper, "Remember, now, you're a dramatic critic." And, lo!
he was no more Dickensy than the merest penny-a-liner.
This was true to some extent of Walt Whitman and certainly was true of Edgar Allan Poe. (The strangest people,
it will be observed, have put in some time as dramatic
critics; such people, for instance, as Eugene Field and

Richard Harding Davis and Edward Bok and Elihu Root).
Probably they were all verbose.

Yet I suspect it could be demonstrated that the most
telling of all dramatic criticisms have found expression in
less than fifty words. Also that the best of all were never
written at all. To substantiate this, I have been raking my
memory for the ones that have lodged there while longer
and more majestical utterances have faded out of mind as
completely as though they had never been written.

What we are looking for, of course, is the happy sentence that speaks volumes. As an example, consider the
familiar problem presented by the players who can do
everything on the stage except act. I have in mind a still
celebrated beauty to whom that beauty opened wide the
stage-door full thirty years ago. Since then she has devoted
herself most painstakingly to justifying her admission. She
has keen intelligence and great industry. She has learned
every trick of voice and gesture that can be taught. She
has acquired everything except some substitute for the in-
born gift. Something to that effect, expressed, of course, as
considerately as possible, ought, it seems to me, to be a part
of any report on her spasmodic reappearances.

It usually takes about five hundred words. Yet Mr. Cohan
managed it pretty well in a single sentence when he was
passing on a similar case in one of his own companies. An
attempt was made to argue with him that the veteran actor
under review was a good fellow and all that. "He's a fine
fellow, all right," Cohan assented amiably enough, and then
added, with murderous good-humor, "There's really only
one thing I've got against him. He's stage-struck."

You see, often the perfections of these capsule criticisms
are achieved by mere bluntness—are arrived at by the no
more ingenious process than that of speaking out in meeting. I was struck with that on the melancholy occasion

when John and Ethel Barrymore lent a momentary and delusive glamour to a piece called "Clair de Lune" by Michael Strange, the exquisitely beautiful poetess whom Mr. Barrymore had just married. By the time its third act had unfolded before the pained eyes of its first audience, there was probably not a single person in that audience who was not thinking that, with all the good plays lying voiceless on the shelf, Michael Strange's shambling and laboriously *macabre* piece would scarcely have been produced had it not been for the somewhat irrelevant circumstance of her having married Mr. Barrymore, the surest means, apparently, of engaging his priceless services for one's drama. Now, some such opinion, I say, was buzzing in every first-night head. All the critics thought just that. Yet they all described nervous circles around this central idea, dancing skittishly about it as though it had been a Maypole. Full of what Gladys Unger was once inspired to call "a dirty delicacy," reluctant, perhaps, to acknowledge the personal equation in criticism, and weighed down, probably, by an ancient respect for the marriage tie, they avoided all audible speculation as to why Mr. Barrymore had put the piece on at all. All, that is, except one. Mr. Whittaker of "The Chicago Tribune"—the same Mr. Whittaker, by the way, who married the fair Ina Claire— cheerfully put the prevailing thought into three devastating words. He entitled his review: "For the Love of Mike."

That is not the only time I have seen the very essence and spirit of a review distilled in a single head-line. It happened on the occasion when the late Sir Herbert Tree, ever and always recognized behind the most ornate make-ups, ever and always himself through all faint-hearted efforts at disguise, appeared for the first time in London in "The Merchant of Venice." It was on that occasion that his more illustrious brother, Max Beerbohm, then merely the

dramatic critic of "The Saturday Review," went backstage to felicitate the star but was overlooked in the crush
of notables who were crowding around. When Tree chided
him afterwards for unfraternal neglect, Max murmured:
"Ah, I was there but you did not know me in your beard."
Of course Max could not write the review of his own
brother's performance—a task delegated, therefore, to John
Palmer, whose comment on the play was awaited, naturally
enough, with considerable interest. Palmer wrote a polite,
though mildly derisive, review of the production and entitled it: "Shylock as Mr. Tree."

I find that the crispest reviews which come back in
this effort at memory have taken many forms. For instance, when it was quite the leading American sin to
attend the agitating performances of "Sapho" by Olga
Nethersole, Franklin P. Adams made his comment in one
quatrain:

> I love little Olga,
>   Her plays are so warm.
> And if I don't see them
>   They'll do me no harm.

The late Charles Frohman, on the other hand, was likely
to sum up plays most felicitously in telegrams. Once, when
he was producing an English comedy at his cherished
Empire Theater in New York, he received just after the
première a cable of eager, though decently nervous, inquiry from the author in London, who could not bear to
wait until the reviews and the box-office statements reached
him. "How's it going?" was the inquiry. Frohman cabled
back: "It's gone."

Of course, many of the best capsule criticisms are classics.
There was Warren's tart comment on Joe Jefferson's performance as *Bob Acres* in "The Rivals," a brilliant feat of
comedic genius made out of whole cloth, so little origin did

it have in the rôle as originally written. "Ha!" quoth Warren, "Sheridan twenty miles away." And there was the fe-
line stroke usually ascribed to Wilde—the one which said
that Tree's *Hamlet* was funny without being vulgar. And
there was the much-quoted knifing of still another *Hamlet* by an unidentified bandit who said, after the performance, that it would have been a fine time to settle the great
controversy as to who wrote the play: one need merely
have watched beside the graves of Shakespere and Bacon
to see which one turned over.

Fairly familiar, also, are two ascribed by tradition to
Eugene Field, in the days when he was dramatic critic of
"The Denver Post" and used to go to the once-famous
Tabor Grand to see "Modjesky ez Cameel," the days when
the peak of the season for him was marked by the engage-
ment of a vagrant, red-headed soubrette named Minnie
Maddern. Of one performance of "Hamlet" there, Field's
entire review consisted of two short melancholy sentences.
He wrote: "So-and-so played Hamlet last night at the
Tabor Grand. He played it till one o'clock." And it was
Field who haunted the declining years of Creston Clarke
with his review of that actor's *Lear*. Clarke, a journeying
nephew of Edwin Booth, passed through Denver and gave
there a singularly unimpressive and unregal performance
in that towering tragedy. Field couldn't bear it and finally
vented his emotions in one sentence. Said he: "Mr. Clarke
played the King all evening as though under constant fear
that some one else was about to play the Ace."

Of course some beautiful capsule criticisms are doomed
to a lesser fame because it is so difficult to detach them
from their circumstances and their context. This is true,
for instance, of several deft summaries by Heywood Broun.
When some years ago one Butler Davenport put on a
juvenilely obscene little play at his own little theater in

New York, Broun scowled and wrote, "Some one should spank young Mr. Davenport and take away his piece of chalk." Then there was the hilarious episode which grew out of the production for one afternoon in the spring of 1917 of Wedekind's "Frühlingserwachen," which Broun translated as "The Spring Offensive." In his little piece on the subject, he mentioned casually that to his mind an actor named Stein gave in the leading rôle the worst performance he had ever seen on any stage. Stein sued for damages, but the court decided, after some diverting testimony, that after all a critic was free to express his esthetic judgment, however incompetent, or however painful it might prove to the subject. Later it became Mr. Broun's embarrassing duty to review another performance by the same aggrieved Stein in another play. Broun evaded the duty until the last sentence, where he could have been found murmuring, "Mr. Stein was not up to his standard."

I am inclined to think, however, that the best of the tabloid reviews have been oral. Coleridge's famous comment on Kean's *Hamlet*—that seeing it was like reading Shakespere by flashes of lightning—was said by him but written by somebody else, wasn't it? Certainly the two best of my day were oral criticisms. One was whispered in my ear by a comely young actress named Tallulah Bankhead, who was sitting incredulous before a deliberate and intentional revival of Maeterlinck's "Aglavaine and Selysette," a monstrous piece of perfumed posturing, meaning exactly nothing. Two gifted young actresses and a considerable bit of scenery were involved, and much pretentious rumbling of voice and wafting of gesture had gone into the enterprise. Miss Bankhead, fearful, apparently, lest she be struck dead for impiety, became desperate enough to whisper, "there is less in this than meets the eye."

The other was tossed off by that delightful companion and variegated actor, Beerbohm Tree. Hurrying from California to New York, he joined at the eleventh hour the already elaborated rehearsals of "Henry VIII," into which he was to step in the familiar scarlet of *Wolsey*. He was expected to survey whatever had been accomplished by his delegates and pass judgment. He approved cheerfully enough of everything until he came to the collection of damsels that had been dragged into the theater as ladies in waiting to the queen. He looked at them in pained and prolonged dissatisfaction and then said what we have all wanted to say of the extra-women in nearly every throne-room and ball-room and school-room scene since the theater began. "Ladies," said Tree, peering at them plaintively through his monocle, "just a little more virginity, if you don't mind."

TWO BUMS HERE WOULD SPEND FREELY EXCEPT FOR POVERTY

by John McNulty

John McNulty is the Bard of Third Avenue, the poet who sings of the people who come into the Third Avenue bars for a beer or a shot, or to place a two-buck bet with one of the local bookies. Like Runyon, Kober, and others, McNulty has chosen a small area and made it his own, and nobody can write about his area as well as he can.

NOBODY KNOWS how the boss of this saloon on Third Avenue reaches such quick decisions about people who come in, but he does. Like in the case of the two bums who came in Sunday afternoon off the avenue.

It was that time on Sunday afternoon that the inhabitants of this place call the Angelus. That's about four o'clock when late hangovers from Saturday night come in one by one. They stay that way, too, one by one. Each man makes himself into an island, standing in front of the bar, and everyone keeps a space on each side of him the way water is on the sides of islands. These hangovers feel too terrible to talk to each other for a couple of hours yet, anyway. Each of them keeps staring into the mirror in back of the bar and saying to himself, "Look at you, you'll never amount to anything. You went to school and grew up and everything and now look at you, you'll never amount to anything." Old veteran Third Avenue bartenders call this fighting the mirror, and they all think it is very bad for a man. The place is sad and quiet when a batch of hangovers are doing this and so someone nicknamed this time of Sunday afternoon the Angelus.

The boss was tending bar himself. He was on the pledge again this Sunday afternoon, so he was standing behind the bar and not saying hardly anything. He is a sour man when not drinking, because he is a man who doesn't take very well to not drinking.

The two bums came in walking as if they had the bottoms of rocking chairs for feet. They had that heel-and-toe walk that punch-drunk fighters have that roll from heels to toes like a rocking chair rocks from back to front. They were never fighters, though, these two bums, too frail-built and no cauliflower ears on them.

They were scratch bums. In this neighborhood they call them scratch bums when they've got as far low as they could get, and don't even try any more to keep themselves without bugs on them. Therefore, scratch bums.

One bum had a version of a straw hat on him he rescued, most likely out of a ash can in a fashionable neighborhood. It had onetime been one of those peanut straws they call them that look like a panama that's got sunburned, only cheaper price. The hat had a hell of a swaggering big brim on it, and looked funny over the scratch bum's crummy clothes. The other bum carried a closed cigar box under one arm, for God knows what and nobody ever did find out. The two bums were arm in arm and they came in without making hardly a sound.

The boss took a drag on his cigarette and laid it down,

the way he does when he's ready to tell bums to turn right around and get out of there, but the bums reached the bar before he did that. They come rolling up to the bar on the rocking-chair feet and one bum, the most sad-faced one, dredged up two nickels out of his pocket and slithered them onto the bar.

"How much is a glass of wine?" the bum asked, and even the hangovers heard him and looked surprised. Nobody ever asks for a glass of wine hardly in that neighborhood. Except maybe on Christmas Eve some nondrinker might unloosen himself up that much on account of Christmas. They keep wine only for show-off, so when the bum asked for wine a couple of the hangovers looked at him and so did the boss. He didn't seem to believe his ears, but he answered the bum. "Aw, wine is twenty-five cents," the boss said. He shoved back the puny pair of nickels at the bum.

"Oh!" the bum said. Just plain "Oh." He picked up his two nickels and him and his pal turned to go out. They took a couple steps toward the door when all of a sudden the boss yelled, "Hey, just a minute!" and wiggled a finger on one hand for them to come back to the bar.

Well, the two bums stood there, wondering what was going to happen. The boss walked down to the other end of the bar and he reached back and got two of the best wineglasses and wiped the dust off of them. He walked back with a hell of a flourish and set the glasses on the bar in front of the two bums. In this place they keep the imported stuff that's hard to get on account of there's a war in a little locker under the back end of the bar. The boss stalked back to this locker and out he hauls a bottle of imported Spanish sherry. Not the junk, a bottle of the McCoy, the real stuff, best in the house. He went to the bums and poured out two glasses full. Then he said, "Drink up, fellers, and welcome!"

You'd think the bums might be surprised, but they didn't look it. They seemed to take it in their stride like everything else. They lifted the glasses and drank the wine slow.

"Thank you, sir," the one with the big-brim hat said. "We won't be botherin' you any longer." And the two of them give their mouths a slow swipe with the backs of their hands and swivelled around from the bar and walked out. The bums looked dignified.

"Now, why in the hell did you do that?" one of the hangovers asked the boss.

"Never mind why I done it," the boss said, grumpy. "Those fellers would spend thousands of dollars if it wasn't for they haven't got even a quarter. Only two nickels. Never mind why I done it."

The boss kept smoking his cigarette a while and paying no attention to the hangover customers. After a couple minutes, damn if he didn't go down again to the far end of the bar and get his hat. He kept trying it on this way and that in front of the mirror.

"I wish to God," he said, "I could get my hat to set on my head the way that hat set on the bum. Now, didn't it have a hell of a jaunty look to it?"

THE SNATCHING OF BOOKIE BOB

by Damon Runyon

Now it comes on the spring of 1931, and what with times being very tough indeed, a number of prominent Broadway citizens become very active in the kidnaping dodge. Among these are three characters from Brooklyn named Harry the Horse, Spanish John, and Little Isadore, and when the finger is put on a guy named Bookie Bob. . . .

But there's no point in trying to tell you about it when it's a well-known fact that no one can tell a Runyon-type story (which is a story about Broadway and gangsters and horse-players) as well as Damon Runyon, although hundreds of imitators have tried.

Ladies and gentlemen, we take you back to the early days of Repeal in a masterpiece by the author of *Butch Minds the Baby, Tight Shoes, Lady for a Day,* and other modern classics—the man on whose stories the hit musical, *Guys and Dolls,* is based.

Now it comes on the spring of 1931, after a long hard winter, and times are very tough indeed, what with the stock market going all to pieces, and banks busting right and left, and the law getting very nasty about this and that, and one thing and another, and many citizens of this town are compelled to do the best they can.

There is very little scratch anywhere and along Broadway many citizens are wearing their last year's clothes and have practically nothing to bet on the races or anything else, and it is a condition that will touch anybody's heart.

So I am not surprised to hear rumors that the snatching of certain parties is going on in spots, because while snatching is by no means a high-class business, and is even considered somewhat illegal, it is something to tide over the hard times.

Furthermore, I am not surprised to hear that this snatching is being done by a character by the name of Harry the Horse, who comes from Brooklyn, and who is a character who does not care much what sort of business he is in, and who is mobbed up with other characters from Brooklyn such as Spanish John and Little Isadore, who do not care what sort of business they are in, either.

In fact, Harry the Horse and Spanish John and Little Isadore are very hard characters in every respect, and there is considerable indignation expressed around and about when they move over from Brooklyn into Manhattan and start snatching, because the citizens of Manhattan feel that if there is any snatching done in their territory, they are entitled to do it themselves.

But Harry the Horse and Spanish John and Little Isadore pay no attention whatever to local sentiment and go on the snatch on a pretty fair scale, and by and by I am hearing rumors of some very nice scores. These scores are not extra large scores, to be sure, but they are enough to keep the wolf from the door, and in fact from three different doors, and before long Harry the Horse and Spanish John and Little Isadore are around the race-tracks betting on the horses, because if there is one thing they are all very fond of, it is betting on the horses.

Now many citizens have the wrong idea entirely of the

snatching business. Many citizens think that all there is
to snatching is to round up the party who is to be snatched
and then just snatch him, putting him away somewhere
until his family or friends dig up enough scratch to pay
whatever price the snatchers are asking. Very few citizens
understand that the snatching business must be well organized and very systematic.

In the first place, if you are going to do any snatching,
you cannot snatch just anybody. You must know who
you are snatching, because naturally it is no good snatching
somebody who does not have any scratch to settle with.
And you cannot tell by the way a party looks or how he
lives in this town if he has any scratch, because many a
party who is around in automobiles, and wearing good
clothes, and chucking quite a swell is nothing but the
phonus bolonus and does not have any real scratch whatever.

So of course such a party is no good for snatching, and
of course guys who are on the snatch cannot go around
inquiring into bank accounts, or asking how much this
and that party has in a safe-deposit vault, because such
questions are apt to make citizens wonder why, and it is
very dangerous to get citizens to wondering why about
anything. So the only way guys who are on the snatch can
find out about parties worth snatching is to make a connection with some guy who can put the finger on the right
party.

The finger guy must know the party he fingers has plenty
of ready scratch to begin with, and he must also know that
this party is such a party as is not apt to make too much
disturbance about being snatched, such as telling the gen-
darmes. The party may be a legitimate party, such as a
business guy, but he will have reasons why he does not
wish it to get out that he is snatched, and the finger must

know these reasons. Maybe the party is not leading the right sort of life, such as running around with blondes when he has an ever-loving wife and seven children in Mamaroneck, but does not care to have his habits known, as is apt to happen if he is snatched, especially if he is snatched when he is with a blonde.

And sometimes the party is such a party as does not care to have matches run up and down the bottom of his feet, which often happens to parties who are snatched and who do not seem to wish to settle their bill promptly, because many parties are very ticklish on the bottom of the feet, especially if the matches are lit. On the other hand, maybe the party is not a legitimate guy, such as a party who is running a crap game or a swell speakeasy, or who has some other dodge he does not care to have come out, and who also does not care about having his feet tickled.

Such a party is very good indeed for the snatching business, because he is pretty apt to settle without any argument. And after a party settles one snatching, it will be considered very unethical for anybody else to snatch him again very soon, so he is not likely to make any fuss about the matter. The finger guy gets a commission of twenty-five per cent of the settlement, and one and all are satisfied and much fresh scratch comes into circulation, which is very good for the merchants. And while the party who is snatched may know who snatches him, one thing he never knows is who puts the finger on him, this being considered a trade secret.

I am talking to Waldo Winchester, the newspaper scribe, one night and something about the snatching business comes up, and Waldo Winchester is trying to tell me that it is one of the oldest dodges in the world, only Waldo calls it kidnaping, which is a title that will be very repulsive to guys who are on the snatch nowadays. Waldo Winchester claims that hundreds of years ago guys are around snatching parties, male and female, and holding them for ransom, and furthermore Waldo Winchester says they even snatch very little children and Waldo states that it is all a very, very wicked proposition.

Well, I can see where Waldo is right about it being wicked to snatch dolls and little children, but of course no guys who are on the snatch nowadays will ever think of such a thing, because who is going to settle for a doll in these times when you can scarcely even give them away? As for little children, they are apt to be a great nuisance, because their mamas are sure to go running around hollering bloody murder about them, and furthermore little children are very dangerous, indeed, what with being apt to break out with measles and mumps and one thing and another any minute and give it to everybody in the neighborhood.

Well, anyway, knowing that Harry the Horse and Spanish John and Little Isadore are now on the snatch, I am by no means pleased to see them come along one Tuesday evening when I am standing at the corner of Fiftieth and Broadway, although of course I give them a very jolly hello, and say I hope and trust they are feeling nicely.

They stand there talking to me a few minutes, and I am very glad indeed that Johnny Brannigan, the strong-arm cop, does not happen along and see us, because it will give Johnny a very bad impression of me to see me in such company, even though I am not responsible for the company. But naturally I cannot haul off and walk away from this company at once, because Harry the Horse and Spanish John and Little Isadore may get the idea that I am playing the chill for them, and will feel hurt.

"Well," I say to Harry the Horse, "how are things going, Harry?"

"They are going no good," Harry says. "We do not beat a race in four days. In fact," he says, "we go overboard today. We are washed out. We owe every bookmaker at the track that will trust us, and now we are out trying to raise some scratch to pay off. A guy must pay his bookmaker no matter what."

Well, of course this is very true, indeed, because if a guy does not pay his bookmaker it will lower his business standing quite some, as the bookmaker is sure to go around putting the blast on him, so I am pleased to hear Harry the Horse mention such honorable principles.

"By the way," Harry says, "do you know a guy by the name of Bookie Bob?"

Now I do not know Bookie Bob personally, but of course I know who Bookie Bob is, and so does everybody else in this town that ever goes to a race-track, because Bookie Bob is the biggest bookmaker around and about, and has plenty of scratch. Furthermore, it is the opinion of one and all that Bookie Bob will die with this scratch, because he is considered a very close guy with his scratch. In fact, Bookie Bob is considered closer than a dead heat.

He is a short fat guy with a bald head, and his head is always shaking a little from side to side, which some say is a touch of palsy, but which most citizens believe comes of Bookie Bob shaking his head "No" to guys asking for credit in betting on the races. He has an ever-loving wife, who is a very quiet little old doll with gray hair and a very sad look in her eyes, but nobody can blame her for this when they figure that she lives with Bookie Bob for many years.

I often see Bookie Bob and his ever-loving wife eating

in different joints along in the Forties, because they seem to have no home except a hotel, and many a time I hear Bookie Bob giving her a going-over about something or other, and generally it is about the price of something she orders to eat, so I judge Bookie Bob is as tough with his ever-loving wife about scratch as he is with everybody else. In fact, I hear him bawling her out one night because she has on a new hat which she says costs her six bucks, and Bookie Bob wishes to know if she is trying to ruin him with her extravagances.

But of course I am not criticizing Bookie Bob for squawking about the hat, because for all I know six bucks may be too much for a doll to pay for a hat, at that. And furthermore, maybe Bookie Bob has the right idea about keeping down his ever-loving wife's appetite, because I know many a guy in this town who is practically ruined by dolls eating too much on him.

"Well," I say to Harry the Horse, "if Bookie Bob is one of the bookmakers you owe, I am greatly surprised to see that you seem to have both eyes in your head, because I never before hear of Bookie Bob letting anybody owe him without giving him at least one of their eyes for security. In fact," I say, "Bookie Bob is such a guy as will not give you the right time if he has two watches."

"No," Harry the Horse says, "we do not owe Bookie Bob. But," he says, "he will be owing us before long. We are going to put the snatch on Bookie Bob."

Well, this is most disquieting news to me, not because I care if they snatch Bookie Bob or not, but because somebody may see me talking to them who will remember about it when Bookie Bob is snatched. But of course it will not be good policy for me to show Harry the Horse and Spanish John and Little Isadore that I am nervous, so I only speak as follows:

"Harry," I say, "every man knows his own business best, and I judge you know what you are doing. But," I say, "you are snatching a hard guy when you snatch Bookie Bob. A very hard guy, indeed. In fact," I say, "I hear the softest thing about him is his front teeth, so it may be very difficult for you to get him to settle after you snatch him."

"No," Harry the Horse says, "we will have no trouble about it. Our finger gives us Bookie Bob's hole card, and it is a most surprising thing, indeed. But," Harry the Horse says, "you come upon many surprising things in human nature when you are on the snatch. Bookie Bob's hole card is his ever-loving wife's opinion of him.

"You see," Harry the Horse says, "Bookie Bob has been putting himself away with his ever-loving wife for years as a very important guy in this town, with much power and influence, although of course Bookie Bob knows very well he stands about as good as a broken leg. In fact," Harry the Horse says, "Bookie Bob figures that his ever-loving wife is the only one in the world who looks on him as a big guy, and he will sacrifice even his scratch, or anyway some of it, rather than let her know that guys have such little respect for him as to put the snatch on him. It is what you call psychology," Harry the Horse says.

Well, this does not make good sense to me, and I am thinking to myself that the psychology that Harry the Horse really figures to work out nice on Bookie Bob is tickling his feet with matches, but I am not anxious to stand there arguing about it, and pretty soon I bid them all good evening, very polite, and take the wind, and I do not see Harry the Horse or Spanish John or Little Isadore again for a month.

In the meantime, I hear gossip here and there that Bookie Bob is missing for several days, and when he finally shows up again he gives it out that he is very sick during his absence, but I can put two and two together as well as anybody in this town and I figure that Bookie Bob is snatched by Harry the Horse and Spanish John and Little Isadore, and the chances are it costs him plenty.

So I am looking for Harry the Horse and Spanish John and Little Isadore to be around the race-track with plenty of scratch and betting them higher than a cat's back, but they never show up, and what is more I hear they leave Manhattan and are back in Brooklyn working every day handling beer. Naturally this is very surprising to me, because the way things are running beer is a tough dodge just now, and there is very little profit in same, and I figure that with the scratch they must make off Bookie Bob, Harry the Horse and Spanish John and Little Isadore have a right to be taking things easy.

Now one night I am in Good Time Charley Bernstein's little speak in Forty-eight Street, talking of this and that with Charley, when in comes Harry the Horse, looking very weary and by no means prosperous. Naturally I gave him a large hello, and by and by we get to gabbing together and I ask him whatever becomes of the Bookie Bob matter, and Harry the Horse tells me as follows:

Yes [Harry the Horse says], we snatch Bookie Bob all right. In fact, we snatch him the very next night after we are talking to you, or on a Wednesday night. Our finger tells us Bookie Bob is going to a wake over in his old neighborhood on Tenth Avenue, near Thirty-eighth Street, and this is where we pick him up.

He is leaving the place in his car along about midnight, and of course Bookie Bob is alone as he seldom lets anybody ride with him because of the wear and tear on his car cushions, and Little Isadore swings our flivver in front of him and makes him stop. Naturally Bookie Bob is greatly surprised when I poke my head into his car and tell him

I wish the pleasure of his company for a short time, and at first he is inclined to argue the matter, saying I must make a mistake, but I put the old convincer on him by letting him peek down the snozzle of my John Roscoe.

We lock his car and throw the keys away, and then we take Bookie Bob in our car and go to a certain spot on Eighth Avenue where we have a nice little apartment all ready. When we get there I tell Bookie Bob that he can call up anybody he wishes and state that the snatch is on him and that it will require twenty-five G's, cash money, to take it off, but of course I also tell Bookie Bob that he is not to mention where he is or something may happen to him.

Well, I will say one thing for Bookie Bob, although everybody is always weighing in the sacks on him and saying he is no good—he takes it like a gentleman, and very calm and businesslike.

Furthermore, he does not seem alarmed, as many citizens are when they find themselves in such a situation. He recognizes the justice of our claim at once, saying as follows:

"I will telephone my partner, Sam Salt," he says. "He is the only one I can think of who is apt to have such a sum as twenty-five G's cash money. But," he says, "if you gentlemen will pardon the question, because this is a new experience to me, how do I know everything will be okay for me after you get the scratch?"

"Why," I say to Bookie Bob, somewhat indignant, "it is well known to one and all in this town that my word is my bond. There are two things I am bound to do," I say, "and one is to keep my word in such a situation as this, and the other is to pay anything I owe a bookmaker, no matter what, for these are obligations of honor with me."

"Well," Bookie Bob says, "of course I do not know you

gentlemen, and, in fact, I do not remember ever seeing any of you, although your face is somewhat familiar, but if you pay your bookmaker you are an honest guy, and one in a million. In fact," Bookie Bob says, "if I have all the scratch that is owing to me around this town, I will not be telephoning anybody for such a sum as twenty-five G's. I will have such a sum in my pants pocket for change."

Now Bookie Bob calls a certain number and talks to somebody there but he does not get Sam Salt, and he seems much disappointed when he hangs up the receiver again.

"This is a very tough break for me," he says. "Sam Salt goes to Atlantic City an hour ago on very important business and will not be back until tomorrow evening, and they do not know where he is to stay in Atlantic City. And," Bookie Bob says, "I cannot think of anybody else to call to get this scratch, especially anybody I will care to have know I am in this situation."

"Why not call your ever-loving wife?" I say. "Maybe she can dig up this kind of scratch."

"Say," Bookie Bob says, "you do not suppose I am chump enough to give my ever-loving wife twenty-five G's, belonging to me, do you? I give my ever-loving wife ten bucks per week for spending money," Bookie Bob says, "and this is enough scratch for any doll, especially when you figure I pay for her meals."

Well, there seems to be nothing we can do except wait until Sam Salt gets back, but we let Bookie Bob call his ever-loving wife, as Bookie Bob says he does not wish to have her worrying about his absence, and tells her a big lie about having to go to Jersey City to sit up with a sick Brother Elk.

Well, it is now nearly four o'clock in the morning, so we put Bookie Bob in a room with Little Isadore to sleep, although, personally, I consider making a guy sleep with

Little Isadore very cruel treatment, and Spanish John and I take turns keeping awake and watching out that Bookie Bob does not take the air on us before paying us off. To tell the truth, Little Isadore and Spanish John are somewhat disappointed that Bookie Bob agrees to settle so promptly, because they are looking forward to tickling his feet with great relish.

Now Bookie Bob turns out to be very good company when he wakes up the next morning, because he knows a lot of race-track stories and plenty of scandal, and he keeps us much interested at breakfast. He talks along with us as if he knows us all his life, and he seems very nonchalant indeed, but the chances are he will not be so nonchalant if I tell him about Spanish John's thought.

Well, about noon Spanish John goes out of the apartment and comes back with a racing sheet, because he knows Little Isadore and I will be wishing to know what is running in different spots although we do not have anything to bet on these races, or any way of betting on them, because we are overboard with every bookmaker we know.

Now Bookie Bob is also much interested in the matter of what is running, especially at Belmont, and he is bending over the table with me and Spanish John and Little Isadore, looking at the sheet, when Spanish John speaks as follows:

"My goodness," Spanish John says, "a spot such as this fifth race with Questionnaire at four to five is like finding money in the street. I only wish I have a few bobs to bet on him at such a price," Spanish John says.

"Why," Bookie Bob says, very polite, "if you gentlemen wish to bet on these races I will gladly book to you. It is a good way to pass away the time while we are waiting for Sam Salt, unless you will rather play pinochle?"

"But," I say, "we have no scratch to play the races, at least not much."

"Well," Bookie Bob says, "I will take your markers, because I hear what you say about always paying your bookmaker, and you put yourself away with me as an honest guy, and these other gentlemen also impress me as honest guys."

Now what happens but we begin betting Bookie Bob on the different races, not only at Belmont, but at all the other tracks in the country, for Little Isadore and Spanish John and I are guys who like plenty of action when we start betting on the horses. We write out markers for whatever we wish to bet and hand them to Bookie Bob, and Bookie Bob sticks these markers in an inside pocket, and along in the late afternoon it looks as if he has a tumor on his chest.

We get the race results by 'phone off a poolroom downtown as fast as they come off, and also the prices, and it is a lot of fun, and Little Isadore and Spanish John and Bookie Bob and I are all little pals together until all the races are over and Bookie Bob takes out the markers and starts counting himself up.

It comes out then that I owe Bookie Bob ten G's, and Spanish John owes him six G's, and Little Isadore owes him four G's, as Little Isadore beats him a couple of races out west.

Well, about this time, Bookie Bob manages to get Sam Salt on the 'phone, and explains to Sam that he is to go to a certain safe-deposit box and get out twenty-five G's, and then wait until midnight and hire himself a taxicab and start riding around the block between Fifty-first and Fifty-second, from Eight to Ninth Avenues, and to keep riding until somebody flags the cab and takes the scratch off him.

Naturally Sam Salt understands right away that the snatch is on Bookie Bob, and he agrees to do as he is told, but he says he cannot do it until the following night because he knows there is not twenty-five G's in the box and he will

have to get the difference at the track the next day. So there
we are with another day in the apartment and Spanish John
and Little Isadore and I are just as well pleased because
Bookie Bob has us hooked and we naturally wish to wiggle
off.

But the next day is worse than ever. In all the years I
am playing the horses I never have such a tough day, and
Spanish John and Little Isadore are just as bad. In fact,
we are all going so bad that Bookie Bob seems to feel sorry
for us and often lays us a couple of points above the track
prices, but it does no good. At the end of the day, I am in
a total of twenty G's, while Spanish John owes fifteen, and
Little Isadore fifteen, a total of fifty G's among the three of
us. But we are never any hands to hold post-mortems on
bad days, so Little Isadore goes out to a delicatessen store
and lugs in a lot of nice things to eat, and we have a fine
dinner, and then we sit around with Bookie Bob telling
stories, and even singing songs together until time to meet
Sam Salt.

When it comes on midnight Spanish John goes off and
lays for Sam, and gets a little valise off Sam Salt. Then
Spanish John comes back to the apartment and we open the
valise and the twenty-five G's are there okay, and we cut
this scratch three ways.

Then I tell Bookie Bob he is free to go about his business,
and good luck to him, at that, but Bookie Bob looks at me
as if he is very much surprised, and hurt, and says to me
like this:

"Well, gentlemen, thank you for your courtesy, but what
about the scratch you owe me? What about these markers?
Surely, gentlemen, you will pay your bookmaker?"

Well, of course we owe Bookie these markers, all right,
and of course a man must pay his bookmaker, no matter
what, so I hand over my bit and Bookie Bob put down

something in a little notebook that he takes out of his kick.

Then Spanish John and Little Isadore hand over their dough, too, and Bookie Bob puts down something more in the little notebook.

"Now," Bookie Bob says, "I credit each of your accounts with these payments, but you gentlemen still owe me a matter of twenty-five G's over and above the twenty-five I credit you with, and I hope and trust you will make arrangements to settle this at once because," he says, "I do not care to extend such accommodations over any considerable period."

"But," I say, "we do not have any more scratch after paying you the twenty-five G's on account."

"Listen," Bookie Bob says, dropping his voice down to a whisper, "What about putting the snatch on my partner, Sam Salt, and I will wait over a couple of days with you and keep booking to you, and maybe you can pull yourselves out. But of course," Bookie Bob whispers, "I will be entitled to twenty-five per cent of the snatch for putting the finger on Sam for you."

But Spanish John and Little Isadore are sick and tired of Bookie Bob and will not listen to staying in the apartment any longer, because they say he is a jinx to them and they cannot beat him in any manner, shape or form. Furthermore, I am personally anxious to get away because something Bookie Bob says reminds me of something.

It reminds me that besides the scratch we owe him, we forget to take out six G's two-fifty for the party who puts the finger on Bookie Bob for us, and this is a very serious matter indeed, because everybody will tell you that failing to pay a finger is considered a very dirty trick. Furthermore, if it gets around that you fail to pay a finger, nobody else will ever finger for you.

So [Harry the Horse says] we quit the snatching business

because there is no use continuing while this obligation is outstanding against us, and we go back to Brooklyn to earn enough scratch to pay our just debts.

We are paying off Bookie Bob's IOU a little at a time, because we do not wish to ever have anybody say we welsh on a bookmaker, and furthermore we are paying off the six G's two-fifty commission we owe our finger.

And while it is tough going, I am glad to say our honest effort is doing somebody a little good, because I see Bookie Bob's ever-loving wife the other night all dressed up in new clothes, very happy indeed.

And while a guy is telling me she is looking so happy because she gets a large legacy from an uncle who dies in Switzerland, and is now independent of Bookie Bob, I only hope and trust [Harry the Horse says] that it never gets out that our finger in this case is nobody but Bookie Bob's ever-loving wife.

THOUGHTS

by John O'Reilly

Sobering Thought

Adult frolic
Is largely alcoholic.

*Sad Thought by a Tourist Whose Conscience Forces
Him to Visit a Museum Rather than a Night Club*

I admit this is a wonderful world
But I'd prefer a place more liberally girled.

R. TAYLOR

*". . . and now I'm off, taking with me only the bare
necessities of life."*

CHARLES ADDAMS

"Dr. Fairburn is going to tell us about some of his interesting experiences among the hèad-shrinking tribes of Ecuador."

ROBERT DAY

"I'm sorry. This section is reserved for officers."

MORT WALKER

"He is out in back talking politics with the garbage man."

MISCHA RICHTER

"Sorry!"

JEFF KEATE

"Hinkle, was a wallet containing a ticket to Tahiti and ten thousand dollars turned in to you? Hello, where's Hinkle?"

DON TOBIN

*"You mean that's all you have left out of your
week's allowance!"*

SALO ROTH

*"So help me, if he kisses her once more,
I'll never sneak in here again."*

GEORGE PRICE

*"A powerful glass, sir. Looks like I'm right on
top of you, doesn't it?"*

ROY L. FOX

RICHARD DECKER

"May I see your ticket stub?"

IRWIN CAPLAN

*"I'm to entertain you until mother finishes dressing. First
I'll imitate my father imitating your husband coming up
the street at three o'clock in the morning."*

AL ROSS

"Well, what are you staring at?"

VIP (VIRGIL PARTCH)

"Let me know if he bothers you, ma'am."

SYD HOFF

"Jeffery's insanely jealous, aren't you, Jeffery? Jeffery!"

CLYDE LAMB

HENRY SYLVERSON

TOM HUDSON

"You Rang, sir?"

ERNEST MARQUEZ

"So you're the Willie Dresser who lost all that money at a poker game the other night?"

YVONNE

by Frank Sullivan

One of your editors has been haunted for several years by a small boy who stands in front of his window at dinnertime each evening and shouts, apparently to nobody in particular, "Git them varmints, pardner." Your editor has thrown various things at the boy—bricks, bottles, shoes, and once even another small boy, who lived in an adjoining apartment and had fallen into the habit of leaning out of his window and shouting, "Drop that jet, Space Cadet!"—but the menace still persists.

You can see, then, why your editor was immediately in favor of Frank Sullivan's piece, which deals with a small girl with a bass voice and a yearning for someone named Yvonne. Nor was it difficult to convince your other editor. Though not haunted by small boys or girls, he has a man who comes into the courtyard of his building every night at nine, laughs three short laughs— like this: Ha! Ha! Ha!—and goes away until the next night.

Frank Sullivan is also the creator of the famous Cliché Expert.

EVERY afternoon at three o'clock a little girl with a deep bass voice appears at the corner of Beekman Place and Fifty-First Street and shouts "Yvonne!" for an hour and a half. On Saturdays she starts in the morning.

Apparently she wants to get in touch with another little

girl named Yvonne, although I admit this is only one man's opinion. Up to now, Yvonne has not, to the best of my knowledge and belief, given any sign of responsiveness, and, frankly, I am worried.

At first I didn't care whether Yvonne answered or not. Then I hoped she wouldn't, just to spite the little girl. But now I want her to answer. More than anything else in the world I want Yvonne to answer that little girl, so that I can pick up the threads of my disordered life and try to make a new start.

I do not know how long the little girl with the bass voice has been on that corner shouting "Yvonne!" This is my third winter in this neighborhood and I do not think she was shouting it the winter of 1930–1931, although I wouldn't want to say for sure, because that was the winter the little boy was shouting "Glurk!" and I was working on the glurk case to the exclusion of all other interests. She might have been shouting "Yvonne!" and it just might not have registered with me. Your ear does acquire a certain selectivity about noises after you have lived in New York since January 6, 1919, and particularly after you have worked in newspaper city rooms from January 7, 1919, to February 27, 1931.

My guess would be that she has been at it a considerable length of time, judging from the obvious condition of her vocal chords. Because even the fact that she is out on that corner in all kinds of weather shouting "Yvonne!" could not account for her present voice. Even if her mother had been frightened by a fire siren, it wouldn't account for it. A little girl certainly not more than ten or eleven does not develop a voice like Bert Lahr's unless she has been shouting "Yvonne!" or something for a long time.

Furthermore, it is plain she is no novice at shouting. She has a technique that would do credit to a Wagnerian soprano. When she shouts "Yvonne!" she accents the first syllable and holds it, crescendo, for as long as thirty seconds. (I've clocked her on this.) Then she gives you the "vonne," in pear-shaped tones audible for about two of our city blocks.

The little boy who glurked had no particular technique. He just traveled up and down Beekman Place shouting "Glurk! Glurk! Glurk!" in a voice which, although of a treble appropriate to his years (he was about seven), had a curiously carrying quality. Now I defy anybody with a spark of curiosity in his makeup to sit by idly without wondering why even a *little* boy should want to spend the better part of his waking hours shouting "Glurk!" I dropped everything and went out gunning for the little codger. After several unsuccessful forays, I found him one day, lurking in the wake of a vasty beldame who came sailing down East Fifty-First Street laden to the gunwales with groceries.

He had a stick, whittled into something approaching a resemblance to a rifle. He would aim the stick at her, cock an eye, make a trigger motion with his finger, and say "Glurk!"

"Playing, little boy?" I asked, pleasantly.

He regarded me suspiciously.

"Is that a gun?" I pursued ingratiatingly.

"Yes," he conceded. He was pretty short with me, too.

"My goodness, don't tell me you're shooting that lady with it!"

"Aw, she's my mother."

"But don't you know you must never shoot your mother in the back? You should fight fair, and give Mummy a chance to defend herself. Why do you say 'Glurk'?"

"Aw, that's the noise when the gun shoots," he explained, with impatience.

"Did you ever hear of a Maxim silencer?" I asked.

He hadn't. I explained that it was a gadget that eliminated the glurk in guns. Then I asked him if he thought it would be worth while to accept a retainer of fifty cents a week to put a Maxim silencer on his gun. He accepted.

"But there's one condition," I warned him. "When I'm up there in that apartment, trying to work to keep body and soul together, every time I hear a glurk out of you, off comes three cents from the fifty. Remember, now."

The first week he owed me sixteen cents. The second week he wiped that out and made two cents. The third week he made twenty-three cents. The next week he collected the full half-dollar, and the week after that he demanded a raise of ten cents.

Thus, at a trifling cost, I had not only abolished glurking on our block, but I had also taught that little shaver a lesson in self-control and thrift, and at a formative age when it was apt to do him the most good. Not to mention the fact that when he grows up, if he should decide to take up a career of crime, he will, thanks to me, know how to use a Maxim silencer.

I would like to be of some similar service to the little girl who shouts "Yvonne!" but, damn it all, I can't *catch* her.

Every afternoon when school is out, I make ready to dart down to the corner at the first shout of "Yvonne!" but no matter how fast I get down those twelve flights, she's gone when I reach the street. As soon as I get back to the apartment, she's at it again.

She's a fool to elude me because, if she only knew it, I'd be an eager and valuable lieutenant. She's got me completely sold on the idea of locating Yvonne. I never was so bent on anything in my life. I'll bet you Carnegie would snap me up if he were alive and on the corner of Beekman Place and Fifty-First Street shouting "Yvonne!" Carnegie was a canny old party. The secret of his success was his ability to pick the right lieutenants.

I could help the little girl in lots of ways. I could help her shout "Yvonne!" and I could shout it at hours when she does not have access to the corner, such as three o'clock in the morning. How does she know that three o'clock in the morning isn't the very time to reach Yvonne? I tried it at half-past two the other morning, but when I stood on the corner and called for Yvonne, two taxicab-drivers, a door-man, and a cop responded and none of them would admit he was Yvonne.

Maybe it would help if we organized Beekman Place to help in the search for Yvonne. I could do that and it would not be difficult, because, thank God, the old husking-bee spirit has not disappeared from our little community. No Beekmanite in distress is suffered to go for long unaided. Outsiders may call it parochialism, but we have another name for it. We call it Loyalty. We of Beekman Place are a simple, rugged people without any frills. Life is no bed of roses for us. The soil is rocky, the climate none too salubri-ous, and the East River, which is our outlet to the sea (and the secret of our greatness), is full of floating tomato cans. But we eke out an existence on our little rock over here. It was good enough for our grandfathers, and at least we can look any man in the face, which is more than most of our critics from the effete tribes of western Manhattan can do. And we have given three Presidents to the country: Millard Fillmore, Guthrie McClintic, and Katharine Cor-nell.

But enough of braggadocio.

I thought that if everybody on Beekman Place would gather *en masse* on the Fifty-First Street corner on a day to be known as Find Yvonne for the Little Girl Day and then, at a given signal, set up a community roar for Yvonne, the resulting hullabaloo might fetch her, because I'm sure that with all our talent over here, we must have some mighty good Yvonne-shouters among us. If that uproar didn't fetch Yvonne, then I think we could fairly assume that nothing ever will; that she is a myth. We can then take her little friend aside and explain gently that there is no use shouting "Yvonne!" any more; that, in fact, it is henceforth taboo on Beekman Place.

After that, if she shouts for Yvonne again, we can throw her into the East River for breaking the taboo. This may seem harsh, but it is the law of the tribe and it will be for the common good.

ADVENTURES WITH THE ANGELS

by H. Allen Smith

If you happen to be a serious student of spiritualism, you won't be amused by the selection which follows. Your editors, however, are not believers in the spirit world (the only ghosts we've seen are those on our television screens)—and we found "Adventures with the Angels" hilarious.

H. Allen Smith, who explores the spirit world with a cynical eye in this selection, is, of course, the ex-newspaperman who rose to rapid fame as the screwball's Boswell with his book, *Low Man on a Totem Pole.* He has since examined more screwballs and others in *Life in a Putty-Knife Factory,* from which this selection was taken, and in a number of other books.

SPIRITUALISM—the belief that a living human being can gabble back and forth with the dead—is one of the most delightful frauds mankind has put upon himself. I have a sincere envy for those people who honestly believe in spiritualism because they must surely have a lot of fun.

I'd like very much to be able to talk with Thorne Smith, if only to ask him if he's getting enough to drink. I'd give up radio if, at will, I could tune in Grandpa Smith, the last Czar of Russia (he'd have to talk English), Giacomo Casanova, Hitler's papa, Noah, Fatty Arbuckle, Lola Montez, and Adam.

If I could get in touch with these people and others I might mention, and if I could spend my evenings talking with them, I'd never have to worry about material for books. I could get a complete book that probably would retail at $3.50 or maybe even $5.00 in a limited signed edition out of Adam alone, if he'd talk. I mean if he *could* talk. Maybe that's why the spiritualists have never brought Adam through. He never stayed around long enough to learn the language, and I'm pretty certain he wouldn't know how to write on a slate. If I could acquire this spiritualistic ability, problems such as that involving Adam's means of communication would come up, but I'd handle them someway. I attended a séance once in which Otto H. Kahn came through and talked in Italian dialect. This was all the more remarkable because Otto H. Kahn, at that sitting, was still alive. So if he could emerge from the spirit planes and chat with me in Italian dialect, surely Adam, considering all the time he's been out there, should be able to talk something.

I attended my first séance soon after I arrived in New York, back in 1929. The medium was a Negro woman, and after she had brought back sundry kinsfolk for the customers, she came through with a horse. No question about it. A man in the audience spoke up and said that he'd like to communicate with a dear horse he once owned—a horse named Edna. Within thirty seconds there was a heavy clumping about the dark room and then the man who had asked for Edna let out a sharp cry. Edna had given him an affectionate kick on the shin.

For a couple of years after that I almost lived at séances, always attending them in the company of Joseph Dunninger. Dunninger is the man who offers a fortune in cash to any spiritualistic medium he cannot expose or debunk.

Dunninger was for years one of the leading American magicians, and I always liked him because he never pulled a half dollar out of my nose. I have a nose that is large enough to hold perhaps $6.50 in half dollars and I have known other magicians who have embarrassed me in public by reaching up and pulling large objects out of it, including hard-boiled eggs. Dunninger never pesters his friends with such stuff.

One of the chief ghost-conjurers of that period in New York was a little Italian named Nino Pecararo. He's the one who brought back Otto H. Kahn in Italian dialect. All his spirits, in fact, spoke in dialect. Dunninger and I attended a number of Pecararo's spooky shows. The Italian boy enjoyed a large following because, some years earlier, he had helped convince Sir Arthur Conan Doyle that spiritualism is true.

We were in the elegant apartment of a spiritualistic architect one evening and Nino, concealed in his cabinet, was fetching back spirits as fast as he could talk. It was a lively show, and when it was over, I found myself standing against a wall between two middle-aged women Believers. One of these women turned to me and said:

"Wasn't it *simply* miraculous!"

"No," I said.

Both women came at me then, demanding to know what I meant.

"Well," I said, "I'd never be convinced unless I could be inside that cabinet with him during one of his séances."

It was a foolish thing to say. Before I knew what was going on, another séance had been scheduled for a week later and Nino had agreed that I could enter the cabinet with him. I tried to withdraw, but those women demanded that I go through with the bargain, since I was such a smart aleck, and Dunninger egged me on.

The special séance was held in the office of a Broadway

lawyer and Nino was quietly sullen when he arrived that
night. A goodly crowd was there, including a noted orchestra leader and a society woman with a high-pitched
chest. Nino's wrists and ankles were bound and his body
was placed in a sack of heavy black netting. Then he was
tied securely to a straight-backed chair and placed in the
cabinet. Next they tied me to a chair and settled me alongside Nino, perhaps two feet away from him. The lights were
doused, the people in the audience formed themselves into
a semicircle in front of the cabinet, and the séance began.

Nino and I sat in the darkest darkness I have ever known
and faced a heavy black curtain which separated us from
the audience. The people outside made not a sound, and
Nino scarcely moved a muscle for thirty minutes. During
those thirty minutes my small supply of courage began to
ebb. I started thinking as follows:

"This bastard is crazy. He's crazy and he's mad as hell at
me for presuming to get into this cabinet with him. He's
even crazy enough to kill me. I know he's able to wiggle
himself out of those ropes and out of that sack. He's so mad,
so crazy, that he's going to get loose and pick up that chair
and brain me with it."

My thoughts raced along like that and I started to sweat.
Still no sound from Nino—no audible indication that he
was escaping his bonds. Then, without warning, he let go
with one of the most piercing shrieks ever heard on earth.
It was enough to frighten a fence post. Coming as it did
after that long, awful, black silence, the shriek even scared
the members of the audience out front. And me—I was too
weak and limp to shudder. All the strength drained out of
me and my body, at that moment, didn't possess enough
energy to have put forth a pimple. I just sat there and
waited for him to strike, figuring myself as a sure thing for

the Great Beyond. He let half a minute go by after the shriek, then he spoke:

"That . . . was . . . Theodore . . . Roosevelt."

I didn't believe in spiritualism then, and I don't now, but if that was Theodore Roosevelt, a pox on him. What a thing to do!

For a while I debated the advisability of getting the hell out of that cabinet, but then I thought of the embarrassment of facing the people outside and resolved to stay a bit longer. What followed was another long period of silence. I could hear Nino squirming a bit now and then. This time he'd get me. This time it would be the chair on my head. Those were the longest minutes of my life—about forty of them—and at last it came again. Another shriek, worse than the first. I leaped a foot and a half off the floor, chair and all. Then came Nino's voice again:

"That . . . was . . . King of . . . Italia."

And that was enough for me. They hadn't tied me securely and I managed to get the ropes off. I didn't care any more about the shame of it. I simply got up and parted the curtains and got out of that damned place, away from Theodore Roosevelt and the King of Italia. The people outside understood and were silently sympathetic, and nobody chided me for leaving the cabinet. I simply took a place at the rear and stood there trying to think up a fool-proof murder plan, a way of killing that devil Nino without getting caught.

The spirits that came after that were much less noisy and seemed, in fact, to have a certain jubilation in their voices. Nino began bringing back dead grandmothers and uncles and cousins and the like. My departure from the cabinet had turned him into a spiritualistic ball of fire. Then Ed Wolf, the radio producer, spoke up and asked if he might

have Napoleon Bonaparte on the line. There was a groaning
and grunting inside the cabinet and suddenly Nino came
plunging through the curtains, carrying them with him. He
was free of the chair but still in the net, and he began
threshing about on the floor. He had kicked the legs off two
chairs before someone got the lights switched on. Half-a-
dozen men piled on top of the writhing medium and someone got a bucket of cold water and poured it on him. Then
he quieted down and they cut the net and ropes off him.
Soon he opened his eyes, looked all around, and muttered:

"Whatta happen?"

By good fortune I didn't have a club in my hand, or I'd
have then and there put him into the deepest of all trances.

The spiritualists said that my adventure in the cabinet
disproved nothing. They contended that Teddy Roosevelt
and the King of Italy actually had come back. I was in no
mood to argue with them. I went home.

Subsequently Nino Pecararo confessed himself a fraud.
Dunninger got him to sign a confession in which he admitted that he was nothing more than an escape artist, able
to extricate himself from bonds. The spiritualists answered
this by saying that Dunninger had hypnotized Nino into
making such a confession.

I wrote stories for the United Press about the various
séances I attended and one day J. W. T. Mason came to
me and began questioning me about spiritualism. Mr.
Mason, who died two years ago, was a famous journalist,
author, psychologist, philosopher, and an authority on
Oriental culture. He was a handsome man with tremendous
dignity, much given to deep thinking. He gave me one of
his books, and I still have it though I've never been able
to read it. A dozen times I've lowered my head and plowed
into it, but it's too much for me. I don't even understand
the long inscription he wrote in it for me.

Mr. Mason worked at a desk near my own and, as I say, he became curious about my adventures among the spiritualists. He wanted to know what I thought about the whole thing and I said I thought it was a lot of ordure. He said I should never take such an attitude. He told me how he had spent years studying various religions and he spoke of Keeping an Open Mind. I always liked him and respected him, but he could never put that frightful malady on me—the disease of the Open Mind. He asked me if I would someday take him to a séance. I said I would.

A week or so later Dunninger put on a séance of his own. His idea was to play medium himself for an evening and demonstrate that he, through sheer trickery, could achieve all the manifestations produced by spiritualists, and then some.

I went to Dunninger and told him about Mr. Mason and we cooked up a little plot. Dunninger asked me to dig up some obscure fact out of Mr. Mason's past history—some incident that would likely be forgotten now.

It was a tough job, but after considerable research I came upon an old biographical sketch of J. W. T. Mason which made mention of a youthful journalistic exploit. Mason, it seemed, had attracted international attention around the turn of the century by obtaining an interview with Leopold II of Belgium. The interview was a lengthy affair and dealt chiefly with Leopold's exploitation of the Congo Free State. This was the obscure fact I handed over to Dunninger.

The phony séance was held in a Manhattan office building, and by prearrangement I arrived with Mr. Mason just as the show was about to start. We sat down with the other invited guests and waited. Mr. Mason, you must understand, thought he was attending a real séance.

Dunninger put on a good performance, slopping ectoplasm all over the place, jingling bells, producing raps here

and there, and babbling in half-a-dozen "spirit-control"
voices. Mr. Mason just sat there in the darkness, eagerly
taking it all in. The thing went along for about twenty
minutes and then there was a long silence and, after that,
a heavy, throaty voice came from the black curtains.

"Is Mason present?" it asked.

I could feel my companion tighten up at my side. For a
moment he seemed unable to answer and then, in a
strangely timid voice, he said:

"Which Mason?"

"Mason," said the hollow voice from the cabinet.

"J. W. T. Mason?" asked J. W. T. Mason.

"That is right," said the voice.

"Yes," he called out. "Yes. I'm—yes, this is J. W. T. Mason
speaking."

He sounded as though he had a telephone receiver at his
ear.

"Do you know me, Mason?" came the voice.

Mr. Mason hesitated a long while. He had spent many
years among Englishmen and had acquired certain British
mannerisms of speech which he employed particularly
when under stress.

"No," he finally said. "No, I can't say I do, old man. Who
are you?"

"I am an old friend of yours, Mason. An old, old friend.
Think back. Think far back. You must remember me. You
must remember Leopold."

By now Mr. Mason was sitting on the edge of his chair,
leaning forward, taut as a banjo string.

"Haw!" he said.

The ghostly voice continued:

"Do you remember, Mason, the long talk we had? Do
you remember?"

"Haw!" from Mr. Mason.

"Can you remember, Mason, what we talked about?"

"Haw!" A long pause. "Yes, Your Highness, I remember quite well. It was—" The voice from the cabinet interrupted him.

"Yes," it said, "it was about the Congo. It was a good long talk and I wish—I wish . . ." The voice began to grow faint and then, fading away, concluded: ". . . and I wish we could continue it."

"Haw!" said Mr. Mason. The voice had faded into what sounded like the indistinct mumblings of an old man, then there was quiet in the room, and the lights came on. I had to act quickly. Mr. Mason was sitting there on the edge of his chair, blinking, and appeared to be in some sort of a trance himself.

"Come on," I said, seizing him by the arm. "Let's get out of here."

We were in the corridor and headed for the street by the time Dunninger had emerged from the cabinet.

"Extraordinary!" Mr. Mason kept saying as we walked down the street. Then he'd crinkle up his brow and puff furiously at a cigarette and think. At the corner he mumbled a good night and got into a cab.

When I reached the office the following day I noted that he was not at his desk. I explored around and finally found him. He was standing at a window, staring out over Brooklyn, smoking, thinking. He stood there for half an hour, then he began to pace up and down the office. Several times he started toward me as though to ask me a question. Then he'd change his mind and resume his pacing, or go back to the window and stare out at eternity (which is over Brooklyn).

I let the thing go on for a couple of hours and then I decided I'd better tell him. He was worrying himself sick. Perhaps he was now faced with the prospect of revising his whole philosophy, calling in all his books and doing them over. He had to be told, so I told him.

He'd have been justified in picking up the nearest copy spike and letting me have it, but he didn't. He put on his spectacles, which he wore attached to a black ribbon, and stared at me for a long time, and then he grinned.

"I couldn't puzzle it out," he said. "The peculiar thing— the amazing thing—was that voice. It was exactly like Leopold's voice. Haw!"

The Mason adventure came in 1930, and while I attended a few séances after that I soon lost touch with spiritualistic matters. Then in 1941, when I was engaged on a brief career as a syndicated columnist, I wrote a piece kidding the ghost-grabbers. An avalanche of mail came down upon me. The letters arrived from spiritualists all over the United States and not a single one of them denounced me. A columnist who attacks dogs or chrysanthemums or stamp collectors or Abbott & Costello will get mail that is filled with bitter invective. Yet the spiritualists startled me by their serenity. Their letters could be divided into two groups— those attempting to prove through personal experience that spiritualism is true, and those containing the following theme:

"You poor boy! You are simply deluded. God has not made the way clear to you. If you could only understand! If you could only see! And you will someday. You will see the light!"

In the former category was, for example, a letter from a lady in St. Louis. She wrote:

All my life I have been told what was coming to pass by falling into a trance and see it come. I saw the war start and saw the Japs take control of the world. Conan Doyal appeared to me while I was sitting in the Odean Theater. Once I was alone in bed in my apartment when I heard a slight movement in the next room and sat up in bed, and there in the next room was a big black man dressed in black from head to heels and was looking at me as though awaiting my orders. One look was enough for me, but I was not so frightened but what I re-membered what to say to dismiss him, and I lost no time in saying: "Depart in the name of the Lord Jesus Christ and come no more." And he was gone. My life has been so full of these visions that I am used to them.

I'm glad I don't have them because I'd never get used to them. I don't want that black guy around my house, night or day, and I don't want Conan "Doyal" getting in the way when I'm looking at a movie, and, most important of all, I don't want to see any Japs taking control of the world.

As another consequence of that column I wrote about spiritualism, somebody in San Francisco sent me a sub-scription to a weekly newspaper called the New York *Spiritualist Leader*. It was a lively periodical and I enjoyed every issue I got.

The *Leader's* star reporter for a while was Elbert Hub-bard (1856–1915). Mr. Hubbard in 1942 was writing a weekly piece from the spirit world, dictating it to one Irene Remillard, a medium. He said that he had organized a Universary Defense Program with himself as chairman of the board of directors. All the members of this board were "out there" with Mr. Hubbard and among them was Wil-liam T. Stead, who went down on the *Titanic*.

Another contributor to the paper was Will Rogers (1879–1935). Will turned out his column through "automatic writ-ing" translated by a lady in Charlotte, Michigan. He soon ousted Elbert Hubbard as star of the *Leader* staff and, just as it happens to earth newspapermen, Will's success went to his head. He started out writing a column of normal length, but before long his stuff was running into two full columns of type and then three. I remember that one of his pieces contained an apology for repeated delays in getting his copy to the editor. Will explained that he had been extremely busy lately. Said he'd been hanging around Washington, D.C., quite a bit. With Abraham Lincoln.

While I looked forward to reading the post-posthumous writings of Elbert Hubbard and Will Rogers each week, I also enjoyed the workings of a new institution, "The Spiritual Post Office for Earth." This department in the *Leader* was conducted by a medium named Alexander DeChard. Mr. DeChard places an "untreated blank white card" between slates and waits five minutes for the letter to be written. People in the spirit world can write home regularly to their friends and relatives through this, shall we say, dead-letter office? If you want to get in touch with a spirit, you can write in and Mr. DeChard will send your letter along, somehow, and later you will get your answer, if they can locate the party.

Some of the sample letters from out yonder were printed in the *Leader*. One of them was to Wilbur from Lillian. She told all about how it felt when she woke up after dying. Said she smelled flowers. After that, she wrote, she saw Mr. Bruce (a spirit) and his eyes were still troubling him. Then she went to her own funeral, and liked it, though she admitted that she felt sad.

Another letter was from a Deacon Jones, addressed to some kinsfolk in Hartford, Connecticut. Deacon Jones wrote his spirit letter in Negro dialect. From it I quote:

It is necessary dat all ob de people should know de truf about coming back. I ask you, be you gwine to allow yourselves to be so extemporaneously bigoted in dis ere fashion? Am I here or is I not? Why so when you see de glorious cause of Nature when you can't see da beauties ob dis Spiritualism? Open the doors in your heart, Robert! Your brother is here, also Mama, Papa, Lillian, Celia, George West, and Rev. White. All send love.

Sure sounds convincing, doesn't it? Of course I didn't see the original as canceled by Postmaster DeChard. The original, according to de *Leader*, came on a decorative letterhead. At the top was "a psychic picture of the handsome colored deacon in gray and green." The gray was the deacon, no doubt, and the green was his dialect.

TWENTY-FIVE BY CERF

A Selection of Bennett Cerf Jokes

Just about everybody today has stopped believing Milton Berle's picture of himself as a joke-stealer. The actual facts, of course, are that Berle employs a very large crew of gag writers, and that he himself is the most swiped-from and imitated comic in the business.

Not so many people, however, have stopped going along with another self-derider, Bennett Cerf, who constantly pictures himself as building his immensely successful anthologies of jokes with nothing more than a paste pot and a pair of scissors. You can bet it isn't as simple as all that. The secret of the success of Cerf's joke books is that he rewrites and rephrases every joke completely, removing its staleness and making it funny all over again. We recognized a number of old friends, for example, in the twenty-five jokes that follow, but their Cerf-manufactured clothing and fresh wording made them as hilarious to us as if we'd never heard them before.

Your editors, incidentally, have no explanation of how Cerf—who is president of Random House and The Modern Library; a columnist in both *The Saturday Review* and *This Week* Magazine; a frequent panelist and guest on various television shows; editor of play, cartoon, and other anthologies; and compiler of books of jokes—manages to do as much as he does. We suspect there are actually five Bennett Cerfs, each equipped with the energy of three men.

A RACE track habitué told his wife, "The darnedest thing happened to me at Jamaica this afternoon. I was bending down to tie my shoelace and some nearsighted goon strapped a saddle on me."

"What did you do?" asked the wife.

"What the hell could I do?" complained the husband. "I came in third."

The pastor finished a forceful sermon on the Ten Commandments. One parishioner was crushed momentarily, but soon perked up. "Anyway," he told himself, "I have never made a graven image."

Luigi and Vincente made a solemn pact that the one who died first would make every effort to make contact with the one left on earth. Luigi was the first to go, and for months Vincente waited in vain for a word or a sign.

One day, however, as he was walking down a side street, he heard a low, "Vincente, my friend! It's Luigi." He peered frantically in every direction, but the only living thing in sight was a spindly, underfed horse, hitched to a dilapidated ice wagon. "Yeah," said the horse sadly. "It's me, Luigi! Live as long as you can, Vincente, for see what happens when you die! This pig Giuseppe who owns me beats me, starves me, and makes me lug this ice wagon around sixteen hours a day!" "But, Luigi," protested Vincente, "you can talk. Why don't you raise hell with Giuseppe?" "S-s-s-h," cautioned Luigi. "For God's sake don't let him know I can talk. He'll have me hollering 'Ice!'"

A man and his wife were sitting together in the living room one evening. The phone rang and the man answered. He said, on the phone, "How on earth should I know? Why don't you call the Coast Guard?" Then he hung up and returned to his newspaper.

The wife asked, "Who was that, dear?"

The husband said, "I haven't the faintest idea. Some silly jerk wanted to know if the coast was clear."

A guard from a lunatic asylum rushed up to a farmer on the road and said, "I am looking for an escaped lunatic. Did he pass this way?"

The farmer puffed thoughtfully on his corncob pipe and asked, "What does he look like?"

"He's very short," said the guard, "and he is very thin and he weighs about three hundred and fifty pounds."

The farmer looked at him in amazement. "How can a man be short and thin and still weigh three hundred and fifty pounds?" he asked.

"Don't act so surprised," said the guard angrily. "I told you he was crazy."

The famous comedian, Harry Lauder, according to legend, was coming out of the stage door of the Palace Theatre one afternoon when a lady stepped into his path, shook a coin box under his nose, and reminded him, "This is tag day for the hospital fund. Give till it hurts." "Madame," Mr. Lauder told her with a tremor in his voice, "the verra idea hurts."

Two taciturn Maine farmers met each other every morning for twenty years in the village post office without exchanging a single word. One day, Farmer Billings turned left when he exited instead of right. "Where ya goin'?" asked his startled neighbor. "None o' yer durn business," snapped Billings. "And I wouldn't tell yer that much if yer warn't an old friend."

A chap had been complaining to an acquaintance in his office that he was having no luck finding attractive women to take out. His friend said, "I know just the thing for you. Drive up late one afternoon to Westport, and wait at the station for the train to pull in. The wives will be waiting to drive their husbands home, and there are always one or two husbands who miss the train. Ask one of the girls for a date, and she'll be so mad at her husband for failing to appear that she'll be glad to accept."

The man thought this a grand idea, and the very next day he started driving to Connecticut. He was quite excited and impatient, and when he got to Stamford, he thought, "Why should I go any farther? There's a station here, and I'll try my luck." So he waited for the train, and sure enough the men got off and drove away with their wives, and one beautiful girl was left over. He walked over to her and asked her to have dinner with him, and she accepted at once. They dined and wined and danced, and went back to her house for another drink or two. Just as matters were approaching a natural conclusion, the husband entered unexpectedly, and started screaming vituperations at his wife. Suddenly his attention was riveted on the man who was trying unsuccessfully to slide out of the back door. "So it's you, you rat," he bellowed. "I told you *Westport,* not Stamford."

The lieutenant on duty at the Fourteenth Precinct Station heard an excited lady's voice over the phone. "Send somebody right over," she shrilled. "There's an enormous gray animal in my garden pulling up cabbages with his tail."

"What's he doing with them?" asked the copper.

"If I told you," said the voice, "you'd never believe me."

Ezekiel Hubbard was running for sheriff in a New Hampshire county and left no stone unturned in his quest for votes. He went from farm to farm canvassing the electorate.

Mrs. Rockwell saw him coming up the lane one afternoon and reached for a broom. "Get off my property, you good-for-nothing loafer," she cried.

"But, Mrs. Rockwell," remonstrated Ezekiel, "I have just come to ask if you'll vote for me for sheriff."

"Sheriff," snorted Mrs. Rockwell. "You ought to be *in* the lockup, not running it. You're a scoundrel and your father was a scoundrel and your grandfather was a scoundrel. Get out of my sight before I take this broom to you."

Ezekiel considered discretion the better part of valor and departed. Before climbing back into his ancient Model T Ford, he pulled out his notebook and entered, after the name of Rockwell, one word: "Doubtful."

A determined-looking gent strode into a Western Union office, dashed off a telegram, and stamped his foot impatiently while the clerk counted the words. "You've got only nine words in this telegram," said the clerk. "You are entitled to one more without extra charge."

Together the man and the clerk reread the telegram which went as follows: "Galumph, galumph, galumph, galumph, galumph, galumph, galumph, galumph, galumph."

"I can't think of another word to add," said the man.

"Why not another galumph?" suggested the clerk.

"Another galumph?" said the man angrily. "That would be silly."

Three girls gathered in a small restaurant for lunch. "I think I'll have a chicken sandwich," said the first one, "with white meat."

"White meat isn't good for a young girl," said the waiter. "Take roast beef."

"O.K.," said the girl. "Roast beef I like."

"Better make it whole wheat," said the waiter. "It's got more vitamins."

The second girl picked corned beef hash. "Don't take that," said the waiter. "It's made up of things that other people leave on their plates. The London broil is what you should take."

"All right," said the second girl. "Make it London broil, and a cup of coffee."

"Coffee," exclaimed the waiter. "You won't sleep a wink tonight. You take a nice glass of fresh buttermilk."

"Very well," said the girl. "London broil and buttermilk it is."

The third girl looked timidly at the waiter. "What do you think I ought to order?" she said.

"How do I know?" said the waiter indignantly. "Who's got time around here to make suggestions?"

A judge eyed his prisoner disapprovingly and said, "Why did you beat your wife?"

"It was a sudden impulse," explained the prisoner.

"Very well," said the judge. "On a sudden impulse, I am going to put you in the cooler for thirty days."

"O.K.," said the prisoner sadly. "But you are certainly putting a crimp in our honeymoon."

A would-be Broadway producer, operating on a shoestring, was interviewing applicants for the heroine's part. One girl delighted him. "You're just what the doctor ordered," he told her. "Right face, right coloring, right voice, everything called for in the part. By the way, what's your salary?"

"Six hundred dollars a week," said the girl.

"Sorry," snapped the producer. "You're too tall."

"I can't imagine," said an indignant lady to an alienist,

"why my family has insisted upon dragging me to see you. What's wrong with my loving pancakes?"

"Nothing at all," agreed the alienist, rather surprised. "I like pancakes myself."

"Goody, goody," said the lady. "You must come up to my house and let me show you my collection. I've got trunks and trunks full of them."

A motorist was pushing his stalled sedan up a hill, perspiring freely and cussing like a trooper. A parson overheard him and remarked, "Swearing, sir, will avail you nothing. Had you tried prayer, your motor might have responded."

"Oh, yeah?" said the motorist. "Let's see you do it, wise guy."

The parson felt he could not sidestep the challenge. Kneeling on the curb, he prayed, "O Lord, make the car of this poor sinner run under its own power." Then he climbed into the front seat and gingerly pressed his foot on the starter. The motor coughed once or twice, and then began to purr as smoothly as the catalogue said it would. The two men listened entranced. "Well, I'll be damned," said the parson.

A London dowager, very hard of hearing, visited her niece in Edinburgh, and went with her to church on Sunday. The deacon at the door eyed her ear trumpet with deep suspicion. He tapped her on the shoulder and reminded her, "One toot and ye're oot!"

The beggar flaunting the "Please Help the Blind" sign looked so forlorn that the lady fished in her bag and handed him a two-dollar bill.

"Sorry, lady," he said. "Two-dollar bills is bad luck. Ain't you got two singles?"

"How did you know it was a two-dollar bill if you're blind?"

"I ain't blind, lady. My partner's blind. It's his day off, so he's gone to the movies and I'm pinch-hittin' for him. Me, I'm a deaf mute."

A captain and a lieutenant were dining at the Stork Club when a corporal entered escorting a ravishingly beautiful damsel. The captain, a Lycanthropist of sorts (Lycanthropist: one who suffers from the delusion that he is a wolf), sent a note to the corporal: "The Lieutenant, who is a Princeton man, and I, who hail from Williams, bet a fin we could guess the college you come from. May we stop at your table and see who was right?"

Back came the reply: "Please don't bother, gentlemen. I am from the Audubon Institute of Ornithology, and I intend to classify this pigeon myself."

A country gentleman with a big valise walked down the railroad track and tapped a busy section hand on the shoulder. "Hey, feller," he asked, "where do I get the Empire State Express?"

"If you don't get off the track," the section hand informed him, "you'll get it square in the behind."

An old tramp sidled up to the back door of a little English tavern called the George and Dragon and beckoned to the landlady. "I ain't had nuthin' to eat for three days," he wheedled. "Would you spare an old man a bite of dinner?"

"I should say not, you good-for-nothing loafer," said the landlady, and slammed the door in his face.

The tramp's face reappeared at the kitchen window. "I was just wonderin'," he said, "if I could 'ave a word or two with George."

Rex Stout, bewhiskered creator of the fabulous detective, Nero Wolfe, was a passenger aboard a crowded Madison Avenue bus one day. An aggressive little man battled his way to Stout's side and, unable to reach a strap, forthwith clutched a strand of the author's beard in a grip of iron. Stout spluttered indignantly for a full block and finally demanded, "Will you kindly take your paws away from my beard?"

"What's the matter, mister?" said the little man. "Are you getting off?"

The man in lower six was snoring lustily. The lady in the next berth tapped on the partition, but he didn't hear her. Finally she banged so loudly that she almost tore it down altogether. Awake at last, the man rubbed his eyes and grumbled surlily, "Nothing doing, lady. I seen you get on."

Mr. Becker's face lit up as he recognized the man who was walking ahead of him down the subway stairs. He clapped the man so heartily on the back that the man nearly collapsed, and cried, "Goldberg, I hardly recognized you. Why, you've gained thirty pounds since I saw you last, and you've had your nose fixed, and I swear you are about two feet taller." The man looked at him angrily. "I beg your pardon," he said in icy tones, "but I do not happen to be Goldberg."

"Aha," said Mr. Becker. "You've even changed your name."

A man received a big check for services rendered, but discovered that it was one cent short. A stickler for detail, he insisted that the discrepancy be repaired and, in due course, received another check for a single penny. He presented it for payment at his bank. The teller examined it closely and asked him, "How would you like this, sir? Heads or tails?"

CHOCOLATE FOR THE WOODWORK

by Arthur Kober

When Arthur Kober's play, *Having a Wonderful Time,* was a
smash success and he bought his mother a mink coat out of the
proceeds, she was understandably proud of him, and refused
to credit the notion that there might be other successful play-
wrights around New York. One day she returned from a party
and told her son about a woman she had met. "Can you imagine
the nerve of her?" she said scornfully. "Telling *me* that *her* son
was a successful playwright!" "What was the woman's name,
Mother?" Kober asked. "Who remembers?" his mother said.
"Schmingsley—Kingsley—something like that."

Kober has had many other successes since then, including the
writing of many fine motion pictures. Most of all, however, he
likes to write, as he did in *Having a Wonderful Time,* about
the residents of the Bronx, and particularly Miss Bella ("Billie")
Gross.

THE DOORBELL rang, but no one in the Gross household
made the slightest move to answer it. It rang again, clearly
and demandingly.

"*Nu?*" yelled Mrs. Gross from the kitchen, where she
was washing the breakfast dishes. "So just because is here
Sunday, is a vacation fa evveybody, ha? Listen the way

it rings the bell—like a regelleh fecktree fomm lomm clocks. So open op the doom, somebody!"

From the bathroom, Bella shouted, "What'sa matter with evveybody arounn here? Are they deef or something? Fa heaven's sakes, can'tcha hear the bell?"

The task of opening the door clearly devolved upon Pa Gross. He angrily threw his newspaper to the floor and got up from his rocker. "Evvey time a persin sits donn to ridd a couple woids in the paper is alluva sunn a big busy here in house. So who is here the soiving goil? Me! . . . Aw right awready!" The last remark was addressed to the clamoring bell. "You can't see I'm coming?"

The man Mr. Gross ushered into the dining room was a study in sartorial splendor. His Panama hat, which he didn't bother to remove, had a band resplendent in many colors. The Palm Beach suit he wore contrasted vividly with his blue shirt, which, together with a blue tie and a carefully folded blue kerchief which peeped from his breast pocket, gave an ensemble effect. Black-and-white sports shoes and purple socks with red vertical stripes completed a dazzling costume. For a moment, Pa stared in wide-eyed wonder at the magnificent stranger, then he sniffed. There was a pervasive odor about the visitor which he quickly identified as turpentine. This, then, must be the long-awaited painter whose magic was going to transform the dingy Gross apartment into a thing of beauty.

"Good munning, good munning!" Pa twinkled at the fashion plate who stood before him. "So you is the paintner the lendludd is sending, no?"

"No! The paintner is woiking fa me." There was implied rebuke in the man's tone. "I'm the *boss* paintner. Wait, I'll give you mine cott." He reached into his inside pocket, whipped out a stained wallet, and from one of its many folds extracted several cards. By this time Mrs. Gross and

Bella were standing beside Pa, and the visitor solemnly presented each of them with a card.

The three Grosses studied the slips of pasteboard in their hands. A good portion of them was taken up by a design of an open can with the name "Eagle" on it. Above this was the phrase "Old Dutch Process" and below it the legend "Employ a Good Painter. Good Painters Use White Lead. White Lead Lasts." There was barely enough room left for the name, Phillip Rudnick, and an address and telephone number.

While the Grosses examined his card, Mr. Rudnick's attention was devoted to their apartment. With his fingers he dug at a flaky wall, peeling huge hunks from it and leaving a white, gaping wound in a vast field of yellow. "Tchk, tchk, tchk!" Phillip Rudnick's oscillating head tacitly rebuked Mr. and Mrs. Gross. "How people can live in such a place! Lookit how is falling donn the wall in liddle pieces." He continued scraping with his fingers. "Some place you got it here! Comes the Boarder Felt and right away you is gung to get a summints!"

"I begya podden!" Bella's voice was hard and chilly. "We happen not to be inarrested in what the Board of Health is gonna do to us. What we happen to be inarrested in is having this here apartment fixed up so that evvey individual or person who comes along won't stick in their two cents' worth of what's wrong with this place. What we wanna know is just what you intend to do regarding the fixing up of this here apartment."

Mr. Rudnick stared at Bella as if seeing her for the first time. Then, turning to Mr. Gross, he said, "The dutter?" Pa nodded. Mr. Rudnick scraped his purple chin with his nails and eyed Bella reflectively. "She is esking what is Rudnick gung to do with this apottment. Listen, lady." He clasped his hands behind his back and rocked on his heels. "You know hommany yirrs is Rudnick in the paintning business? Plenty! You know hommany apottments is Rudnick fixing op? Plenty, believe me!" His voice suddenly became conversational. "I want you should enswer me a question. You a woiking goil?"

"Uf cuss!" sang out Pa Gross.

"So what is your line?" Mr. Rudnick asked.

"I happen to be the privitt seckatary fa a very important pardy who is inclined along financial matters," said Bella.

"Aha, a seckatary! So how you would like if your boss say to you, 'How you gung to write the letter you putting donn by you in the shuthend book? You gung to put the paper in the machine with the left hend udder the right hend? You gung to use by you the liddle pinkie udder the whole hend?' 'What's the diffrince?' you is gung to give the boss an enswer. 'Mine job is to write it fa you the lettiss. If you like mine job, so is O.K. If you don't like it, then you give me the seck. But how I'm doing the job, that's strickly mine business.'" He waved a finger at Bella. "So the same is with Rudnick. How I'm gung to fix by you the apottment, that's strickly mine business."

"He's positiffly got it right!" declared Pa Gross, placing a hand on the visitor's shoulder. "Mr. Rudnick is foist gung to do the paintning job, then we'll complain when he is finndished."

Mrs. Gross felt it her duty to come to her daughter's defence. "Say, what is here—Europe, maybe, a persin dassent tukk a couple woids? She says something, Bella, and right away is evveybody yelling on her 'Sharrop!'" She glowered at the two men. "Cossacks!"

Mr. Rudnick, busy blotting the back of his neck with his handkerchief, ignored this attack. "Oooh," he complained, "is very hot here in house. Look," he said, "why you so

stingy with the winda opening when is here like a regelleh
stove?" He walked to the window and raised it. He looked
down at the street and then, wildly waving his fist, he cried
out, "Hey, you little bestidds, kipp away fomm mine machine, you hear? In two seconds I'll come donnstairs and
I'll fix you good, you tremps, you!" He turned away from the
window and scowled at the Grosses. "A fine neighborhood
you got it here! Some foist-cless gengsters is gung to be the
kits in the stritt. I'm leaving mine uttemobill donnstairs—
mine machine is a Chevvy," he added parenthetically—
"and right away they scretching op by me the machine, the
no-good bummers! Where I am living, on the Concuss, is
O.K. to leave mine machine a whole day on the stritt and
will come no kits to scretch by me the car. But here in this
neighborhood—" A shrug of his shoulders completed his
comment.

"A lotta people I know," said Bella icily, "they ride with
the subway, where they got no worries who scratches up
the cars."

"Excuse me!" Mr. Rudnick's tone was laden with disdain.
"Evveything I say is with her no good. Now is a sin to have
a machine, ha? Today is a paint job in this neighborhood,
temorreh is a paint job in that neighborhood, next day is
a paint job maybe in the Heights. So the boss paintner
shouldn't have a machine? Listen, you think I get maybe
pleasure fomm mine Chevvy? Nah! Is expenses fa ges, is
expenses fa tires, is all the time expenses. You know hommuch it custs me, mine expenses? Plenty! And that's with
you a sin, ha?"

"Parm me," said Bella, somewhat chastened, "but I happen not to be criticizing whether you have a car or you
don't have one. I happen to be criticizing that just because
some little kids are playing arounn on the street and your

car happens to be in the way, that is no excuse you should indulge in vulgarity or to criticize this neighborhood, which we happen to be living in at the present time."

Mr. Rudnick seemed about to say something sharp and cutting, but thought better of it. "Listen," he said, forcing a smile, "in mine house if mine dutter tukked so fresh to a guest, you know what I would give her? Plenty! But what can a persin speck fomm this neighborhood?" Before Bella could find a fitting rejoinder he had whipped out a notebook and pencil. "*Nu*, Rudnick is not here to make spitches. Rudnick is here to see with the paint job." He abandoned the Grosses to inspect the walls. "Paint with stipple finish the whole thing complete," he mumbled as he made notes. "Wash op the cilling, take away the crecks, fix it the loose plester, and don't fegget you should do kelsomine job. With the flurr—scrape, uf cuss, and you should finndish with two coats fomm shelleck." He headed toward the window and noticed the radiator in passing. "Aha, the radiatiss you should silver op. And with the windiss, take loose puddy away, new puddy put in." Mr. Rudnick continued making notes as he walked from room to room. The Gross family trailed after him, and when he ran his fingers along the woodwork all of them followed suit and nodded discerningly.

The procession returned to the dining room. "O.K.," said Mr. Rudnick, snapping his notebook shut. "Mine paintners will come temorreh to fix it by you the apottment. Will be the place brannew. Will be a pleasure to live here." Again his glance encompassed the room, and he seemed to shudder. "Not like is now."

"What about the matter fomm the color?" asked Bella. "We haven't decided yet what should be the color of the apartment."

"A question!" jeered the painter. "What should be the color? Chotruse, uf cuss! You know what is chotruse?"

"Green," Bella said.

Mr. Rudnick pretended he hadn't heard her. "Chotruse is grinn." This was addressed confidentially to Pa. "Go to the best homes. Go to the finest flets on the Concuss, and is oney one color—chotruse! Mine apottment, where I'm living, is strickly chotruse."

"Well, it so happens I got diffrint idears on the subjeck," said Bella. "It so happens that what we want in the line of color is cream walls—"

"Crimm walls!" bellowed Mr. Rudnick. "Is no more stylish crimm walls! You know where you find crimm walls? In the chipp apottments where is living very common pipple. Feh! But go to the Concuss, go even to the Heights, and you know hommany places is chotruse? Plenty!"

"See here," said Bella, "it's our house. Do you mind leaving us fix it the way we like, inasmuch as we are the folks living here and it so happens you are not?"

Mr. Rudnick eyed her steadily for several seconds. He then turned to Mr. Gross and, nodding in Bella's direction, said, "The boss, ha?"

The old man felt obliged to define his daughter's authority. "She's a single goil. When we fix the apottment like she says, maybe will come here some nice boyess—"

"Fa heaven's sakes, Pa!" Bella screamed. "What's his business that I'm single? Must you tell the whole world who comes here about your own daughter's condition?"

"Dope!" Mrs. Gross's shrill voice was also raised in protest. "Why you don't tell him hommuch money we not yet paying the butcher? Why you don't tell him fomm your gold watch in punnshop? Go on, tell your friend evveything fomm the femily, Mr. Tettltale!"

"Sha, sha, sha!" Mr. Rudnick's features now broke into a disarming smile. "O.K., so now I know how is. So will Rudnick make fa you crimm walls just like the dutter wants it. Now is evveybody serrisfied, and I'm seeing you in the munning."

He started for the hallway, but Bella's next question arrested him. "What about the woodwork?" she asked. "I want it should be a chawklit color."

"Ha?" Mr. Rudnick's baffled expression indicated he wasn't sure he had heard her correctly.

"I want the color should have two tones," explained Bella. "I want cream fa the walls and chawklit fa the woodwork."

Mr. Rudnick lifted his Panama hat and daintily scraped his scalp with his little finger. "Chucklit!" he murmured. Replacing his hat, he slowly and deliberately took out his notebook, scribbled something in it and then looked up. "Excuse me," he said. "What kine chucklit you would like fa the woodwoik—Nestle's udder Hoishey's?"

"See here," said Bella, "I take that remark fomm whence it comes."

"Chucklit!" Mr. Rudnick replaced his book, tapped the crown of his gay Panama with his hand, and stalked to the door. As he was about to leave the apartment, he stopped, stared reflectively into space, and then turned around. "Listen, lady," he shouted at Bella, "Rudnick is gung to fix the place just like you say—two tunns, crimm and chucklit! And listen. If you not finding a nice boy after Rudnick is fixing the apottment, you know what you should put in the chucklit woodwoik? Ammints! You hear me—ammints!"

Bella Gross reached into her arsenal of invective for a particularly annihilating reply, but she was too late. Mr. Rudnick was out of the apartment, leaving behind the ringing echo of his voice shouting "Ammints!"

RÉSUMÉ

by Dorothy Parker

Razors pain you;
Rivers are damp;
Acids stain you;
And drugs cause cramp.
Guns aren't lawful;
Nooses give;
Gas smells awful;
You might as well live.

LOVE IS A FALLACY

by Max Shulman

Only one minor consideration marred our full enjoyment of the Max Shulman selection coming up next: the sinister suggestion in its pages that raccoon coats might be returning to the American scene. Lord help us, the thought sends the mind reeling. We're prepared to accept the return of poodle cuts, men's suits with slits in the back, and even ladies' hats that look like church bells and cover all the hair, but the thought of seeing every young man again appear to be about the girth of Sidney Greenstreet is a shade too much to bear.

However. Max Shulman, one of the newer members of the fraternity of top-line humorists, is at his best when discussing the foibles of college life, and he has a genuine gem in "Love Is a Fallacy."

COOL WAS I and logical. Keen, calculating, perspicacious, acute and astute—I was all of these. My brain was as powerful as a dynamo, as precise as a chemist's scales, as penetrating as a scalpel. And—think of it!—I was only eighteen.

It is not often that one so young has such a giant intellect. Take, for example, Petey Bellows, my roommate at the university. Same age, same background, but dumb as an ox.

A nice enough fellow, you understand, but nothing upstairs. Emotional type. Unstable. Impressionable. Worst of
all, a faddist. Fads, I submit, are the very negation of reason.
To be swept up in every new craze that comes along, to
surrender yourself to idiocy just because everybody else
is doing it—this, to me, is the acme of mindlessness. Not,
however, to Petey.

One afternoon I found Petey lying on his bed with an expression of such distress on his face that I immediately
diagnosed appendicitis. "Don't move," I said. "Don't take
a laxative. I'll get a doctor."

"Raccoon," he mumbled thickly.

"Raccoon?" I said, pausing in my flight.

"I want a raccoon coat," he wailed.

I perceived that his trouble was not physical, but mental.
"Why do you want a raccoon coat?"

"I should have known it," he cried, pounding his temples.
"I should have known they'd come back when the Charleston came back. Like a fool I spent all my money for textbooks, and now I can't get a raccoon coat."

"Can you mean," I said incredulously, "that people are
actually wearing raccoon coats again?"

"All the Big Men on Campus are wearing them. Where've
you been?"

"In the library," I said, naming a place not frequented
by Big Men on Campus.

He leaped from the bed and paced the room. "I've got to
have a raccoon coat," he said passionately. "I've got to!"

"Petey, why? Look at it rationally. Raccoon coats are
unsanitary. They shed. They smell bad. They weigh too
much. They're unsightly. They—"

"You don't understand," he interrupted impatiently. "It's
the thing to do. Don't you want to be in the swim?"

"No," I said truthfully.

"Well, I do," he declared. "I'd give anything for a raccoon coat. Anything!"

My brain, that precision instrument, slipped into high gear. "Anything?" I asked, looking at him narrowly.

"Anything," he affirmed in ringing tones.

I stroked my chin thoughtfully. It so happened that I knew where to get my hands on a raccoon coat. My father had had one in his undergraduate days; it lay now in a trunk in the attic back home. It also happened that Petey had something I wanted. He didn't *have* it exactly, but at least he had first rights on it. I refer to his girl, Polly Espy.

I had long coveted Polly Espy. Let me emphasize that my desire for this young woman was not emotional in nature. She was, to be sure, a girl who excited the emotions, but I was not one to let my heart rule my head. I wanted Polly for a shrewdly calculated, entirely cerebral reason.

I was a freshman in law school. In a few years I would be out in practice. I was well aware of the importance of the right kind of wife in furthering a lawyer's career. The successful lawyers I had observed were, almost without exception, married to beautiful, gracious, intelligent women. With one omission, Polly fitted these specifications perfectly.

Beautiful she was. She was not yet of pin-up proportions, but I felt sure that time would supply the lack. She already had the makings.

Gracious she was. By gracious I mean full of graces. She had an erectness of carriage, an ease of bearing, a poise that clearly indicated the best of breeding. At table her manners were exquisite. I had seen her at the Kozy Kampus Korner eating the specialty of the house—a sandwich that contained scraps of pot roast, gravy, chopped nuts, and a dipper of sauerkraut—without even getting her fingers moist.

Intelligent she was not. In fact, she veered in the opposite direction. But I believed that under my guidance she would smarten up. At any rate, it was worth a try. It is, after all, easier to make a beautiful dumb girl smart than to make an ugly smart girl beautiful.

"Petey," I said, "are you in love with Polly Espy?"

"I think she's a keen kid," he replied, "but I don't know if you'd call it love. Why?"

"Do you," I asked, "have any kind of formal arrangement with her? I mean are you going steady or anything like that?"

"No. We see each other quite a bit, but we both have other dates. Why?"

"Is there," I asked, "any other man for whom she has a particular fondness?"

"Not that I know of. Why?"

I nodded with satisfaction. "In other words, if you were out of the picture, the field would be open. Is that right?"

"I guess so. What are you getting at?"

"Nothing, nothing," I said innocently, and took my suitcase out of the closet.

"Where you going?" asked Petey.

"Home for the week end." I threw a few things into the bag.

"Listen," he said, clutching my arm eagerly, "while you're home, you couldn't get some money from your old man, could you, and lend it to me so I can buy a raccoon coat?"

"I may do better than that," I said with a mysterious wink and closed my bag and left.

"Look," I said to Petey when I got back Monday morning. I threw open the suitcase and revealed the huge, hairy, gamy object that my father had worn in his Stutz Bearcat in 1925.

"Holy Toledo!" said Petey reverently. He plunged his hands into the raccoon coat and then his face. "Holy Toledo!" he repeated fifteen or twenty times.

"Would you like it?" I asked.

"Oh yes!" he cried, clutching the greasy pelt to him. Then a canny look came into his eyes. "What do you want for it?"

"Your girl," I said, mincing no words.

"Polly?" he said in a horrified whisper. "You want Polly?"

"That's right."

He flung the coat from him. "Never," he said stoutly.

I shrugged. "Okay. If you don't want to be in the swim, I guess it's your business."

I sat down in a chair and pretended to read a book, but out of the corner of my eye I kept watching Petey. He was a torn man. First he looked at the coat with the expression of a waif at a bakery window. Then he turned away and set his jaw resolutely. Then he looked back at the coat, with even more longing in his face. Then he turned away, but with not so much resolution this time. Back and forth his head swiveled, desire waxing, resolution waning. Finally he didn't turn away at all; he just stood and stared with mad lust at the coat.

"It isn't as though I was in love with Polly," he said thickly. "Or going steady or anything like that."

"That's right," I murmured.

"What's Polly to me, or me to Polly?"

"Not a thing," said I.

"It's just been a casual kick—just a few laughs, that's all."

"Try on the coat," said I.

He complied. The coat bunched high over his ears and dropped all the way down to his shoe tops. He looked like a mound of dead raccoons. "Fits fine," he said happily.

I rose from my chair. "Is it a deal?" I asked, extending my hand.

He swallowed. "It's a deal," he said and shook my hand.

I had my first date with Polly the following evening. This was in the nature of a survey; I wanted to find out just how much work I had to do to get her mind up to the standard I required. I took her first to dinner. "Gee, that was a delish dinner," she said as we left the restaurant. Then I took her to a movie. "Gee, that was a marvy movie," she said as we left the theater. And then I took her home. "Gee, I had a sensaysh time," she said as she bade me good night.

I went back to my room with a heavy heart. I had gravely underestimated the size of my task. This girl's lack of information was terrifying. Nor would it be enough merely to supply her with information. First she had to be taught to *think*. This loomed as a project of no small dimensions, and at first I was tempted to give her back to Petey. But then I got to thinking about her abundant physical charms and about the way she entered a room and the way she handled a knife and fork, and I decided to make an effort.

I went about it, as in all things, systematically. I gave her a course in logic. It happened that I, as a law student, was taking a course in logic myself, so I had all the facts at my finger tips. "Polly," I said to her when I picked her up on our next date, "tonight we are going over to the Knoll and talk."

"Oo, terrif," she replied. One thing I will say for this girl: you would go far to find another so agreeable.

We went to the Knoll, the campus trysting place, and we sat down under an old oak, and she looked at me expectantly. "What are we going to talk about?" she asked.

"Logic."

She thought this over for a minute and decided she liked it. "Magnif," she said.

"Logic," I said, clearing my throat, "is the science of thinking. Before we can think correctly, we must first learn to recognize the common fallacies of logic. These we will take up tonight."

"Wow-dow!" she cried, clapping her hands delightedly.

I winced, but went bravely on. "First let us examine the fallacy called Dicto Simpliciter."

"By all means," she urged, batting her lashes eagerly.

"Dicto Simpliciter means an argument based on an unqualified generalization. For example: Exercise is good. Therefore everybody should exercise."

"I agree," said Polly earnestly. "I mean exercise is wonderful. I mean it builds the body and everything."

"Polly," I said gently, "the argument is a fallacy. *Exercise is good* is an unqualified generalization. For instance, if you have heart disease, exercise is bad, not good. Many people are ordered by their doctors *not* to exercise. You must *qualify* the generalization. You must say exercise is *usually* good, or exercise is good *for most people*. Otherwise you have committed a Dicto Simpliciter. Do you see?"

"No," she confessed. "But this is marvy. Do more! Do more!"

"It will be better if you stop tugging at my sleeve," I told her, and when she desisted, I continued. "Next we take up a fallacy called Hasty Generalization. Listen carefully: You can't speak French. I can't speak French. Petey Bellows can't speak French. I must therefore conclude that nobody at the University of Minnesota can speak French."

"Really?" said Polly, amazed. "*Nobody?*"

I hid my exasperation. "Polly, it's a fallacy. The generalization is reached too hastily. There are too few instances to support such a conclusion."

"Know any more fallacies?" she asked breathlessly. "This is more fun than dancing even."

I fought off a wave of despair. I was getting nowhere with this girl, absolutely nowhere. Still, I am nothing if not persistent. I continued. "Next comes Post Hoc. Listen to this: Let's not take Bill on our picnic. Every time we take him out with us, it rains."

"I know somebody just like that," she exclaimed. "A girl back home—Eula Becker, her name is. It never fails. Every single time we take her on a picnic—"

"Polly," I said sharply, "it's a fallacy. Eula Becker doesn't *cause* the rain. She has no connection with the rain. You are guilty of Post Hoc if you blame Eula Becker."

"I'll never do it again," she promised contritely. "Are you mad at me?"

I sighed. "No, Polly, I'm not mad."

"Then tell me some more fallacies."

"All right. Let's try Contradictory Premises."

"Yes, let's," she chirped, blinking her eyes happily.

I frowned, but plunged ahead. "Here's an example of Contradictory Premises: If God can do anything, can He make a stone so heavy that He won't be able to lift it?"

"Of course," she replied promptly.

"But if He can do anything, He can lift the stone," I pointed out.

"Yeah," she said thoughtfully. "Well, then I guess He can't make the stone."

"But He can do anything," I reminded her.

She scratched her pretty, empty head. "I'm all confused," she admitted.

"Of course you are. Because when the premises of an argument contradict each other, there can be no argument. If there is an irresistible force, there can be no immovable object. If there is an immovable object, there can be no irresistible force. Get it?"

"Tell me some more of this keen stuff," she said eagerly.

I consulted my watch. "I think we'd better call it a night. I'll take you home now, and you go over all the things you've learned. We'll have another session tomorrow night."

I deposited her at the girls' dormitory, where she assured me that she had had a perfectly terrif evening, and I went glumly home to my room. Petey lay snoring in his bed, the raccoon coat huddled like a great hairy beast at his feet. For a moment I considered waking him and telling him that he could have his girl back. It seemed clear that my project was doomed to failure. The girl simply had a logic-proof head.

But then I reconsidered. I had wasted one evening; I might as well waste another. Who knew? Maybe somewhere in the extinct crater of her mind a few embers still smoldered. Maybe somehow I could fan them into flame. Admittedly it was not a prospect fraught with hope, but I decided to give it one more try.

Seated under the oak the next evening I said, "Our first fallacy tonight is called Ad Misericordiam."

She quivered with delight.

"Listen closely," I said. "A man applies for a job. When the boss asks him what his qualifications are, he replies that he has a wife and six children at home, the wife is a helpless cripple, the children have nothing to eat, no clothes to wear, no shoes on their feet, there are no beds in the house, no coal in the cellar, and winter is coming."

A tear rolled down each of Polly's pink cheeks. "Oh, this is awful, awful," she sobbed.

"Yes, it's awful," I agreed, "but it's no argument. The man never answered the boss's question about his qualifications. Instead he appealed to the boss's sympathy. He committed the fallacy of Ad Misericordiam. Do you understand?"

"Have you got a handkerchief?" she blubbered.

I handed her a handkerchief and tried to keep from screaming while she wiped her eyes. "Next," I said in a carefully controlled tone, "we will discuss False Analogy.

Here is an example: Students should be allowed to look at their textbooks during examinations. After all, surgeons have X rays to guide them during an operation, lawyers have briefs to guide them during a trial, carpenters have blueprints to guide them when they are building a house. Why, then, shouldn't students be allowed to look at their textbooks during an examination?"

"There now," she said enthusiastically, "is the most marvy idea I've heard in years."

"Polly," I said testily, "the argument is all wrong. Doctors, lawyers, and carpenters aren't taking a test to see how much they have learned, but students are. The situations are altogether different, and you can't make an analogy between them."

"I still think it's a good idea," said Polly.

"Nuts," I muttered. Doggedly I pressed on. "Next we'll try Hypothesis Contrary to Fact."

"Sounds yummy," was Polly's reaction.

"Listen: If Madame Curie had not happened to leave a photographic plate in a drawer with a chunk of pitchblende, the world today would not know about radium."

"True, true," said Polly, nodding her head. "Did you see the movie? Oh, it just knocked me out. That Walter Pidgeon is so dreamy. I mean he fractures me."

"If you can forget Mr. Pidgeon for a moment," I said coldly, "I would like to point out that the statement is a fallacy. Maybe Madame Curie would have discovered radium at some later date. Maybe somebody else would have discovered it. Maybe any number of things would have happened. You can't start with a hypothesis that is not true and then draw any supportable conclusions from it."

"They ought to put Walter Pidgeon in more pictures," said Polly. "I hardly ever see him any more."

One more chance, I decided. But just one more. There

is a limit to what flesh and blood can bear. "The next fallacy is called Poisoning the Well."

"How cute!" she gurgled.

"Two men are having a debate. The first one gets up and says, 'My opponent is a notorious liar. You can't believe a word that he is going to say.' . . . Now, Polly, think. Think hard. What's wrong?"

I watched her closely as she knit her creamy brow in concentration. Suddenly a glimmer of intelligence—the first I had seen—came into her eyes. "It's not fair," she said with indignation. "It's not a bit fair. What chance has the second man got if the first man calls him a liar before he even begins talking?"

"Right!" I cried exultantly. "One hundred per cent right. It's not fair. The first man has *poisoned the well* before anybody could drink from it. He has hamstrung his opponent before he could even start. . . . Polly, I'm proud of you."

"Pshaw," she murmured, blushing with pleasure.

"You see, my dear, these things aren't so hard. All you have to do is concentrate. Think—examine—evaluate. Come now, let's review everything we have learned."

"Fire away," she said with an airy wave of her hand.

Heartened by the knowledge that Polly was not altogether a cretin, I began a long, patient review of all I had told her. Over and over and over again I cited instances, pointed out flaws, kept hammering away without letup. It was like digging a tunnel. At first everything was work, sweat, and darkness. I had no idea when I would reach the light, or even *if* I would. But I persisted. I pounded and clawed and scraped, and finally I was rewarded. I saw a chink of light. And then the chink got bigger and the sun came pouring in and all was bright.

Five grueling nights this took, but it was worth it. I had made a logician out of Polly; I had taught her to think. My

job was done. She was worthy of me at last. She was a fit
wife for me, a proper hostess for my many mansions, a suitable mother for my well-heeled children.

It must not be thought that I was without love for this
girl. Quite the contrary. Just as Pygmalion loved the perfect
woman he had fashioned, so I loved mine. I decided to ac-
quaint her with my feelings at our very next meeting. The
time had come to change our relationship from academic
to romantic.

"Polly," I said when next we sat beneath our oak, "tonight
we will not discuss fallacies."

"Aw, gee," she said, disappointed.

"My dear," I said, favoring her with a smile, "we have
now spent five evenings together. We have gotten along
splendidly. It is clear that we are well matched."

"Hasty Generalization," said Polly brightly.

"I beg your pardon," said I.

"Hasty Generalization," she repeated. "How can you say
that we are well matched on the basis of only five dates?"

I chuckled with amusement. The dear child had learned
her lessons well. "My dear," I said, patting her hand in a
tolerant manner, "five dates is plenty. After all, you don't
have to eat a whole cake to know that it's good."

"False Analogy," said Polly promptly. "I'm not a cake.
I'm a girl."

I chuckled with somewhat less amusement. The dear
child had learned her lessons perhaps too well. I decided to
change tactics. Obviously the best approach was a simple,
strong, direct declaration of love. I paused for a moment
while my massive brain chose the proper words. Then I
began:

"Polly, I love you. You are the whole world to me, and
the moon and the stars and the constellations of outer space.
Please, my darling, say that you will go steady with me, for

if you will not, life will be meaningless. I will languish. I will refuse my meals. I will wander the face of the earth, a shambling, hollow-eyed hulk."

There, I thought, folding my arms, that ought to do it.

"Ad Misericordiam," said Polly.

I ground my teeth. I was not Pygmalion; I was Franken- stein, and my monster had me by the throat. Frantically I fought back the tide of panic surging through me. At all costs I had to keep cool.

"Well, Polly," I said, forcing a smile, "you certainly have learned your fallacies."

"You're darn right," she said with a vigorous nod.

"And who taught them to you, Polly?"

"You did."

"That's right. So you do owe me something, don't you, my dear? If I hadn't come along you never would have learned about fallacies."

"Hypothesis Contrary to Fact," she said instantly.

I dashed perspiration from my brow. "Polly," I croaked, "you mustn't take all these things so literally. I mean this is just classroom stuff. You know that the things you learn in school don't have anything to do with life."

"Dicto Simpliciter," she said, wagging her finger at me playfully.

That did it. I leaped to my feet, bellowing like a bull. "Will you or will you not go steady with me?"

"I will not," she replied.

"Why not?" I demanded.

"Because this afternoon I promised Petey Bellows that I would go steady with him."

I reeled back, overcome with the infamy of it. After he promised, after he made a deal, after he shook my hand! "The rat!" I shrieked, kicking up great chunks of turf. "You can't go with him, Polly. He's a liar. He's a cheat. He's a rat."

"Poisoning the Well," said Polly, "and stop shouting. I think shouting must be a fallacy too."

With an immense effort of will, I modulated my voice. "All right," I said. "You're a logician. Let's look at this thing logically. How could you choose Petey Bellows over me? Look at me—a brilliant student, a tremendous intellectual, a man with an assured future. Look at Petey—a knothead, a jitterbug, a guy who'll never know where his next meal is coming from. Can you give me one logical reason why you should go steady with Petey Bellows?"

"I certainly can," declared Polly. "He's got a raccoon coat."

THE LADY ON THE BOOKCASE

by James Thurber

What, friends and constant readers of James Thurber are often asked, are the answers to the sinister secret; in Thurber's cartoons? Is, for example, the lady on the bookcase stuffed or just resting up there? What kind of animal, for another thing, is the one that did something to Dr. Millmoss? And what about that man who's had his head sliced off by a sword—is he dead or will the head just snap on again?

For many years, Thurber, asked about these things, just smiled enigmatically and changed the subject. One day, however, in a sudden burst of confidence, he wrote a full account of all the secrets of his artwork, and we're proud to bring you this confession now.

Your editors are fond of stating the obvious fact that no humor anthology is complete without a prose selection by James Thurber, and that an anthology is doubly complete when it contains both a prose selection by Thurber and a cartoon selection by Thurber. This anthology, then, is complete in multiple, since, as you'll note, the Thurber article that follows is garnished with no less than ten of his magnificent and masterful cartoons.

ONE DAY twelve years ago an outraged cartoonist, four of whose drawings had been rejected in a clump by *The New Yorker*, stormed into the office of Harold Ross, editor of the magazine. "Why is it," demanded the cartoonist, "that you reject my work and publish drawings by a fifth-rate artist

"With you I have known peace, Lida, and now you say you're going crazy."

like Thurber?" Ross came quickly to my defense like the true friend and devoted employer he is. "You mean third-rate," he said quietly, but there was a warning glint in his steady gray eyes that caused the discomfited cartoonist to beat a hasty retreat.

With the exception of Ross, the interest of editors in what I draw has been rather more journalistic than critical. They want to know if it is true that I draw by moonlight, or under water, and when I say no, they lose interest until they hear the rumor that I found the drawings in an old trunk or that I do the captions while my nephew makes the sketches.

The other day I was shoving some of my originals around on the floor (I do not draw on the floor; I was just shoving the originals around) and they fell, or perhaps I pushed

Home

them, into five separate and indistinct categories. I have never wanted to write about my drawings, and I still don't want to, but it occurred to me that it might be a good idea to do it now, when everybody is busy with something else, and get it over quietly.

Category No. 1, then, which may be called the Unconscious or Stream of Nervousness category, is represented by "With you I have known peace, Lida, and now you say you're going crazy" and the drawing entitled with simple dignity, "Home." These drawings were done while the artist was thinking of something else (or so he has been assured

"All right, have it your way—you heard a seal bark."

by experts) and hence his hand was guided by the Unconscious which, in turn, was more or less influenced by the Subconscious.

Students of Jung have instructed me that Lida and the House-Woman are representations of the *anima*, the female essence or directive which floats around in the ageless universal Subconscious of Man like a tadpole in a cistern. Less intellectual critics insist that the two ladies are actual persons I have consciously known. Between these two schools of thought lies a discouragingly large space of time

"That's my first wife up there, and this is the *present* Mrs. Harris."

extending roughly from 1,000,000 B.C. to the middle Nineteen Thirties.

Whenever I try to trace the true identity of the House-Woman, I get to thinking of Mr. Jones. He appeared in my office one day twelve years ago, said he was Mr. Jones, and asked me to lend him "Home" for reproduction in an art magazine. I never saw the drawing again. Tall, well-dressed, kind of sad-looking chap, and as well spoken a gentleman as you would want to meet.

Category No. 2 brings us to Freud and another one of those discouragingly large spaces—namely, the space between the Concept of the Purely Accidental and the Theory of Haphazard Determination. Whether chance is capricious

"For the last time, you and your horsie get away from me and stay away!"

or we are all prisoners of pattern is too long and cloudy a subject to go into here. I shall consider each of the drawings in Category No. 2, explaining what happened and leaving the definition of the forces involved up to you. The seal on top of the bed, then ("All right, have it your way—you heard a seal bark"), started out to be a seal on a rock. The rock, in the process of being drawn, began to look like the head of a bed, so I made a bed out of it, put a man and wife in the bed, and stumbled onto the caption as easily and unexpectedly as the seal had stumbled into the bedroom.

The woman on top of the bookcase ("That's my first wife up there, and this is the *present* Mrs. Harris") was originally

"The father belonged to some people who were driving through in a Packard."

designed to be a woman crouched on the top step of a staircase, but since the tricks and conventions of perspective and planes sometimes fail me, the staircase assumed the shape of a bookcase and was finished as such, to the surprise and embarrassment of the first Mrs. Harris, the present Mrs. Harris, the lady visitor, Mr. Harris and me. Before *The New Yorker* would print the drawing, they phoned me long distance to inquire whether the first Mrs. Harris was alive or dead or stuffed. I replied that my taxidermist had advised me that you cannot stuff a woman, and that my physician had informed me that a dead lady cannot support herself on all fours. This meant, I said, that the first Mrs. Harris was unquestionably alive.

"What have you done with Dr. Millmoss?"

The man riding on the other man's shoulders in the bar ("For the last time, you and your horsie get away from me and stay away!") was intended to be standing alongside the irate speaker, but I started his head up too high and made it too small, so that he would have been nine feet tall if I had completed his body that way. It was but the work of thirty-two seconds to put him on another man's shoulders. As simple or, if you like, as complicated as that. The psychological factors which may be present here are, as I have indicated, elaborate and confused. Personally, I like Dr. Claude Thornway's theory of the Deliberate Accident or Conditioned Mistake.

Category No. 3 is perhaps a variant of Category No. 2; indeed, they may even be identical. The dogs in "The father belonged to some people who were driving through in a

"Touché!"

Packard" were drawn as a captionless spot, and the interior with figures just sort of grew up around them. The hippopotamus in "What have you done with Dr. Millmoss?" was drawn to amuse my small daughter. Something about the creature's expression when he was completed convinced me that he had recently eaten a man. I added the hat and pipe and Mrs. Millmoss, and the caption followed easily enough. Incidentally, my daughter, who was 2 years old at the time, identified the beast immediately. "That's a hippotomanus," she said. *The New Yorker* was not so smart. They described the drawing for their files as follows: "Woman with strange animal." *The New Yorker* was nine years old at the time.

"Well, I'm disenchanted, too. We're all disenchanted."

Category No. 4 is represented by perhaps the best known of some fifteen drawings belonging to this special grouping, which may be called the Contributed Idea Category. This drawing ("Touché!") was originally done for *The New Yorker* by Carl Rose, caption and all. Mr. Rose is a realistic artist, and his gory scene distressed the editors, who hate violence. They asked Rose if he would let me have the idea, since there is obviously no blood to speak of in the people I draw. Rose graciously consented. No one who looks at "Touché!" believes that the man whose head is in the air is really dead. His opponent will hand it back to him with profuse apologies, and the discommoded fencer will replace it on his shoulders and say, "No harm done, forget it." Thus the old controversy as to whether death can be made funny is left just where it was before Carl Rose came along with his wonderful idea.

"You said a moment ago that everybody you look at seems to be a rabbit. Now just what do you mean by that, Mrs. Sprague?"

Category No. 5, our final one, can be called, believe it or not, the Intentional or Thought-Up Category. The idea for each of these two drawings just came to me and I sat down and made a sketch to fit the prepared caption. Perhaps, in the case of "Well, I'm disenchanted, too. We're all disenchanted," another one of those Outside Forces played a part. That is, I may have overheard a husband say to his wife, on the street or at a party, "I'm disenchanted." I do not think this is true, however, in the case of the rabbit-headed doctor and his woman patient. I believe that scene and its caption came to me one night in bed. I *may* have got the idea in a doctor's office or a rabbit hutch, but I don't think so.

If you want to, you can cut these drawings out and push them around the floor, making your own categories or applying your own psychological theories; or you can even invent some fresh rumors. I should think it would be more fun, though, to take a nap, or baste a roast, or run around the reservoir in Central Park.

NEW JOE MILLER JOKE BOOK

by Earl Wilson

In an earlier anthology, your editors made the point that, though Earl Wilson is popularly known as the man who became famous because of his erudite discussions of comparative feminine measurements, he is a skillful and clever writer who would eventually have achieved success even if he'd never discovered the fact that boys and girls are different. Faithful readers will recall that we substantiated this thesis with a Wilson selection that wasn't even faintly libidinous.

Well, we're underlining it again with the Wilson prize package that follows: a discussion of top comedians and their art. Kindly note that it contains nary a B—nary a Wilson-specialty B, that is.

MR. ZERO MOSTEL, the youthful but fat, bald, funny-looking comedian, was induced to flee the New York cafés, where he had achieved enormous prosperity, and speed to Hollywood, where even greater loot awaited him. When he walked into the Mocambo in Hollywood, accompanied by his New York confederate, Ivan Black, and sat down to have dinner, he was wearing a $125 suit—the most expensive drapings that had ever hung on his ill-gotten frame.

As the waiter hovered about waiting for his order, Zero

seized a knife, began spreading butter on some bread, and then suddenly started spreading butter on his coat sleeve, right up to the elbow. He buttered his sleeve with the long, sweeping movements of a barber stropping a razor.

Then he stuck out one fat thumb and buttered it, both top and bottom. When it was thoroughly buttered, he stuck the thumb in his mouth and licked the butter off.

At this point Zero seemed to notice for the first time that the waiter was standing there dumb struck, open-mouthed, and unbelieving.

"Whataya staring at?" Zero demanded.

"Nothing," said the waiter meekly.

"Is there something unusual about what I'm doing, or something?" shouted Zero, seemingly in a great rage.

"No-o-o."

"All right then!" thundered Zero. "Go get me some more butter for my thumb!"

The mad Mostel is one of our really natural comedians; he, for example, does one imitation of a coffee percolator boiling over. He does it expertly and hilariously, suggesting that possibly he spent many years studying percolators about to boil over. Most leading night-club comics depend on gags. They have to have a fast mind and a good memory. I think the greatest of these (he is now graduated from the field) is Milton Berle, radio star, movie star, recent star of *Ziegfeld Follies,* producer of Broadway shows on his own, and—incidentally—a millionaire at thirty-five.

When one of his own productions received a panning from Miss Wilella Waldorf, the drama critic, I said to him, "What have you to say to Miss Waldorf?"

"All I have to say to Miss Waldorf," he said, "is that I'll never eat any more of her salad.

"Anyway," he added, "one of the critics was very nice to me."

"In what way?"

"He didn't see it."

Years ago, when he was fighting his way up, Berle was tagged "The Thief of Bad Gags" by Walter Winchell, and this tag has clung. Some rival comedians allege that his code of ethics is as loose as a girdle on Katharine Hepburn. I don't know whether he steals gags or not, but I do know that he can usually deliver a line better than the person who originated it. Sometimes I take Berle around to some night-club opening. Usually they are able to hold the opening anyway. Berle, sitting in the back, will suddenly stand up and start doing a show while the regular entertainer is on. It's a gag with him, and when he's had a couple of laughs, he'll sit down. He's known to be so good that he'll be begged to get up and tell a few jokes. One night at Leon & Eddie's he got up and said he knew that Joey Adams, the comedian then working there, would be using all his jokes the next night. Adams roared out, "I wouldn't steal any of your jokes—because I wouldn't want Bob Hope to sue me."

Berle made a move to begin an ad-lib battle with Adams but thought better of it and waved his hand, indicating the futility of it all. Everybody present was sorry, because it might have been memorable.

The war and the subsequent Gold Rush brought a lot of hecklers into the night clubs, but the comedians had to be careful about their replies, especially when the hecklers were servicemen. Comedian Henny Youngman got off a good line several years ago (I understand it was written for him by Milton Rubin, a Broadway press agent), when he turned on some disturber and remarked, "This is the first time I ever saw one pair of shoes with three heels."

That retort has been good ever since. Jack Waldron pulled a honey of a line one night when he told a noisy drunk, "Let's play horse—I'll be the front end and you just be yourself."

Surely one of the greatest heckler hecklers was the late Jack White. One night when a woman of doubtful reputation insisted on interrupting him while he was doing his turn, he looked at her imploringly and said, "Please, lady, would you like it if I came over where you lived and turned off your red light?"

Frank Tinney is generally credited with the squelch that shamed a guy who threw him a penny—squelched him so thoroughly that the crack became a minor classic, and then a cliché. "There's only one animal," Tinney said, "that throws a scent."

Frank Fay once answered a drunk's shout of "You stink," by saying, "Remember, you're speaking of the man I love."

Bob Hope's supposed to have said first, "Is that your face, or did you block a kick?"

Eddie Davis, the perennial star at Leon & Eddie's, isn't often bothered by hecklers—because he tells them, "The next beer you order, have them put a head on you." He also tells them, "I never forget a face, but in your case I could make an exception."

Berle uses the abrupt, surprise twist. If somebody says, "I'm pleased to meet you," he'll growl, "Why?" If he appears on the stage with a girl, he may say, "Darling, you're beautiful tonight—you look like you just stepped out of *Vogue*—and fell flat on your face. My act was so bad in vaudeville," he'll continue, if given half a chance, and if not, one fourth of a chance will do, "that the mice in the dressing rooms set traps for me. The crowd would shout, 'We want Berle, we want Berle.' And if it hadn't been for the riot squad, they'd have had me."

In his passion to get laughs he'll forget his abhorrence of the gag-stealing reputation that has been thrust upon him, and use one of his oldest gags. "Boy, was Jack Benny funny last night!" he'll say. "I laughed so hard I almost dropped my paper and pencil. What a trip I had coming in from California. I kissed Betty Grable so much my face went right through the picture frame. What a childhood I had! Boy, those were hectic times. And when I say hectic, I mean exciting, because I don't know what hectic means. I won a cup for imitating Charlie Chaplin. It was worth one dollar, and was I proud! I used to take my relatives down to the pawnshop to see it. Have you met my brother Frank? Is he superstitious! He won't work any week that has a Friday in it."

Henny Youngman's standards are also those fast "one-liners," or "two-liners." Not so successful financially as Berle, he is nevertheless a funny man in any theater or night club.

"I had more trouble with my railroad ticket getting here," Youngman will say. "Trouble, trouble everywhere over my ticket. So I finally straightened it out. I bought one. I was working in a wonderful Florida night club. No cover, no minimum, no people. We had a wonderful boss. He used to stab me good night. I had a girl who was so dumb she thought mechanized infantry was a new way of having a baby. She's so ugly that she has circles under her circles. She will never live to be as old as she looks. When snakes get drunk, they see her.

"I went out to see a ball game," he'll say. "But from where I sat the game was only a rumor. I was up so high I was getting spirit messages. When the usher got me halfway up, he said, 'You'll have to go the rest of the way yourself. From here on my nose bleeds.' Finally I say to a guy next to me, 'How do you like the game?' He says, 'What game? I'm flying the mail to Pittsburgh.'"

And there are a few thousand more, amusing if you

haven't heard them. Joe E. Lewis, Jackie Miles, and Danny Thomas are other leading comedians in the night clubs today, but they use considerable special material that isn't so easy to quote. Lewis, who likes to kid around and ad lib while out on the floor, one night said he would sing, "I Want a Girl Just Like the Girl That Married Dear Old Dad." Or that was what he intended to say. Instead he gave as the title "I Want a Girl Just Like the Girl That Married Harry James." The remark brought down the house and he had to employ a couple of writers to give him a song by that title.

Still, one of the best jokes of the last couple of years didn't even come from a comedian, so far as I can determine. It just started floating around the night clubs, and nobody quite knew its origin. A pretty girl, so the story went, met a suitor who wasn't quite satisfied with her clothes and general appearance. He wanted to dress her up in new finery and jewels before taking her out. So he told her to go to Saks Fifth Avenue and buy some dresses; be good to herself, go see the head of the store, tell her who had sent her, pick out three or four things at $300 to $500, and charge them. Go to Tiffany's for some pearls, not more than $5,000 worth. Then go to Jaeckel's for a new mink coat, and charge that. Get a few of those $50 hats at John Frederics' and charge those.

"And then," he said, "when you're all fixed up, call me at PL 7-3131 and I'll take you out."

"Is that your home or office number?" the girl asked.

"It's the candy store," he said. "They'll call me to the phone."

ON THE VANITY OF EARTHLY GREATNESS

by Arthur Guiterman

The tusks that clashed in mighty brawls
Of mastodons, are billiard balls.

The sword of Charlemagne the Just
Is ferric oxide, known as rust.

The grizzly bear whose potent hug
Was feared by all, is now a rug.

Great Caesar's bust is on the shelf,
And I don't feel so well myself!

THE ETIQUETTE OF COURTSHIP

by Donald Ogden Stewart

———

When your editors wrote Donald Ogden Stewart in Paris to ask permission to use a section of his masterpiece of satire, *Perfect Behavior*, in this anthology, Stewart's reply was characteristic: "My answer is a delighted yes, a habit I picked up while working in Hollywood."

Stewart went on to say that he appreciated our enthusiastic comments about his book, "though you probably tell that to all the boys." Actually, our comments were sober truth. *Perfect Behavior* has been one of our favorite books since its publication, and we have probably bought about a dozen copies each, due to the fact that friends have a habit of examining our copies with delight and swiping them.

Perfect Behavior, as you will note, is a subtle burlesque of the dozens of books of etiquette that turn up on the market each year. It is so legitimate appearing at first glance that Foyle's of London, the largest bookstore in the world, solemnly put it on sale in their etiquette section.

———

COURTSHIP IS one of the oldest of social customs, even antedating in some countries such long-established usages as marriage, or the wearing of white neckties with full evening dress. The beginnings of the etiquette of courtship were apparently connected in some way with the custom of "love" between the sexes, and many of the old amatory forms still survive in the modern courtship. It is generally agreed among students of the history of etiquette that when "love" first began to become popular among the better class of younger people they took to it with such avidity that it was necessary to devise some sort of rules for the conduct of formal or informal love-making. These rules, together with various amendments, now constitute the etiquette of courtship.

Suppose, for example, that you are a young gentleman named Richard Roe desirous of entering upon a formal courtship with some refined young girl of fashion. You are also, being a college graduate, engaged in the bond business. One morning there comes into your financial institution a young lady, named Dorothy Doe, who at once attracts your attention by her genteel manners, as exemplified by the fact that she calls the president of your company "father." So many young people seem to think it "smart" to refer to their parents as "dad" or "my old man"; you are certain, as soon as you hear her say "Hello, father" to your employer, that she is undoubtedly a worthy object of courtship.

CORRECT INTRODUCTIONS; HOW TO MAKE THEM

Your first step should be, of course, the securing of an introduction. Introductions still play an important part in social intercourse, and many errors are often perpetrated by those ignorant of *savoir faire* (correct form). When introducing a young lady to a stranger for example, it is not *au fait* (correct form) to simply say, "Mr. Roe, I want you to shake hands with my friend Dorothy." Under the rules of the *beau monde* (correct form) this would probably be done as follows: "Dorothy (or Miss Doe), shake hands with Mr. Roe." Always give the name of the lady first, unless you are introducing some one to the President of the United States, the Archbishop of Canterbury, a member of the nobility above a baron, or a customer. The person who is being "introduced" then extends his (or her) right ungloved hand and says, "Shake." You "shake," saying at the same time, "It's warm (cool) for November (May)," to which the other replies, "I'll say it is."

This brings up the interesting question of introducing two people to each other, neither of whose names you can remember. This is generally done by saying very quickly to one of the parties, "Of course you know Miss Unkunkunk." Say the last "unk" very quickly, so that it sounds like any name from Ab to Zinc. You might even sneeze violently. Of course, in nine cases out of ten, one of the two people will at once say, "I didn't get the name," at which you laugh, "Ha! Ha! Ha!" in a carefree manner several times, saying at the same time, "Well, well—so you didn't get the name— you didn't get the name—well, well." If the man still persists in wishing to know who it is to whom he is being introduced, the best procedure consists in simply braining him on the spot with a club or convenient slab of paving stone.

The "introduction," in cases where you have no mutual friend to do the introducing, is somewhat more difficult but can generally be arranged as follows:

Procure a few feet of stout manila rope or clothes-line, from any of the better-class hardware stores. Ascertain (from the Social Register, preferably) the location of the young lady's residence, and go there on some dark evening about nine o'clock. Fasten the rope across the sidewalk in front of the residence about six inches or a foot from the ground. Then, with the aid of a match and some kerosene, set fire to the young lady's house in several places and retire behind a convenient tree. After some time, if she is at home, she will probably be forced to run out of her house to avoid being burned to death. In her excitement she will fail to notice the rope which you have stretched across the sidewalk and will fall. This is your opportunity to obtain an introduction. Stepping up to her and touching your hat politely, you say, in a well-modulated voice, "I beg your pardon, Miss Doe, but I cannot help noticing that you are lying prone on the sidewalk." If she is well-bred, she will not at first speak to you, as you are a perfect stranger. This silence, however, should be your cue to once more tip your hat and remark, "I realize, Miss Doe, that I have not had the honor of an introduction, but you will admit that you are lying prone on the sidewalk. Here is my card—and here is one for Mrs. Doe, your mother." At that you should hand her two plain engraved calling cards, each containing your name and address. If there are any other ladies in her family —aunts, grandmothers, et cetera—it is correct to leave cards for them also. Be sure that the cards are clean, as the name on the calling card is generally sufficient for identification purposes without the addition of the thumb-print.

When she has accepted your cards, she will give you one of hers, after which it will be perfectly correct for you to assist her to rise from the sidewalk. Do not, however, press your attentions further upon her at this time, but after expressing the proper regret over her misfortune it would be well to bow and retire.

CARDS AND FLOWERS

The next day, however, you should send flowers, enclosing another of your cards. It might be well to write some message on the card recalling the events of the preceding evening—nothing intimate, but simply a reminder of your first meeting and a suggestion that you might possibly desire to continue the acquaintanceship. Quotations from poetry of the better sort are always appropriate; thus, on this occasion, it might be nice to write on the card accompanying the flowers—" 'This is the forest primeval'—H. W. Longfellow," or " 'Take, oh take, those lips away'—W. Shakespeare." You will find there are hundreds of lines equally appropriate for this and other occasions, and in this connection it might be well to display a little originality at times by substituting pertinent verses of your own in place of the conventional quotations. For example—"This is the forest primeval, I regret your last evening's upheaval," shows the young lady in question that not only are you well-read in classic poetry, but also you have no mean talent of your own. Too much originality, however, is dangerous, especially in polite social intercourse, and I need hardly remind you that the floors of the social ocean are watered with the tears of those who seek to walk on their own hook.

Within a week after you have sent the young lady the flowers, you should receive a polite note of thanks, somewhat as follows: "My dear Mr. Roe: Those lovely flowers came quite as a surprise. They are lovely, and I cannot thank you enough for your thoughtfulness. Their lovely fragrance fills my room as I write, and I wish to thank you again. It was lovely of you."

FLOWERS AND THEIR MESSAGE IN COURTSHIP

It is now time to settle down to the more serious business of courtship. Her letter shows beyond the shadow of a figurative doubt that she is "interested," and the next move is "up to you." Probably she will soon come into the office to see her father, in which case you should have ready at hand some appropriate gift, such as, for example, a nice potted geranium. Great care should be taken, however, that it is a plant of the correct species, for in the etiquette of courtship all flowers have different meanings and many a promising affair has been ruined because a suitor sent his lady a buttercup, meaning "That's the last dance I'll ever take you to, you big cow," instead of a plant with a more tender significance. Some of the commoner flowers and their meaning in courtship are as follows:

Fringed Gentian: "I am going out to get a shave. Back at 3:30."

Poppy: "I would be proud to be the father of your children."

Golden-rod: "I hear that you have hay-fever."

Tuberose: "Meet me Saturday at the Fourteenth Street subway station."

Blood-root: "Aunt Kitty murdered Uncle Fred Thursday."

Iris: "Could you learn to love an optician?"

Aster: "Who was that stout party I saw you with in the hotel lobby Friday?"

Deadly Nightshade: "Pull down those blinds, quick!"

Passion Flower: "Phone Main 5-1249—ask for Eddie."

Raspberry: "I am announcing my engagement to Charlie O'Keefe Tuesday."

Wild Thyme: "I have seats for the theatre Saturday afternoon."

The above flowers can also be combined to make different meanings, as, for example, a bouquet composed of three tuberoses and some Virginia creeper generally signifies the following, "The reason I didn't call for you yesterday was that I had three inner tube punctures, besides a lot of engine trouble in that old car I bought in Virginia last year. Gosh, I'm sorry!"

But to return to the etiquette of our present courtship. As Miss Doe leaves the office you follow her, holding the potted plant in your left hand. After she has gone a few paces you step up to her, remove your hat (or cap) with your right hand, and offer her the geranium, remarking, "I beg your pardon, miss, but didn't you drop this?" A great deal depends upon the manner in which you offer the plant and the way she receives it. If you hand it to her with the flower pointing upward it means, "Dare I hope?" Reversed, it signifies, "Your petticoat shows about an inch, or an inch and a half." If she receives the plant in her right hand, it means, "I am"; left hand, "You are"; both hands—"He, she or it is." If, however, she takes the pot firmly in both hands and breaks it with great force on your head, the meaning is usually negative and your only correct course of procedure is a hasty bow and a brief apology.

RECEIVING AN INVITATION TO CALL

Let us suppose, however, that she accepts the geranium in such a manner that you are encouraged to continue the acquaintance. Your next move should be a request for an invitation to call upon her at her home. This should, above all things, not be done crudely. It is better merely to suggest your wish by some indirect method such as, "Oh—so you live on William Street. Well, well! I often walk on William Street in the evening, but I have never called on any girl there—*yet*." The "yet" may be accompanied by a slight raising of your eyebrows, a wink, or a friendly nudge with your elbow. Unless she is unusually "dense" she will probably "take the hint" and invite you to come and see her some evening. At once you should say, "*What* evening? How about *to-night?*" If she says that she is already engaged for that evening, take a calendar out of your pocket and remark, "Tomorrow? Wednesday? Thursday? Friday? I really have no engagements between now and October. Saturday? Sunday?" This will show her that you are really desirous of calling upon her and she will probably say, "Well, I think I am free Thursday night, but you had better telephone me first."

THE ETIQUETTE OF TELEPHONING

On Thursday morning, therefore, you should go to a public telephone-booth in order to call the young lady's house. The etiquette of telephoning is quite important and many otherwise perfectly well-bred people often make themselves conspicuous because they do not know the correct procedure in using this modern but almost indispensable invention. Upon entering the telephone-booth, which is located, say, in some drug store, you remove the receiver from the hook and deposit the requisite coin in the coin box. If you live in an area which uses the operator rather than dial system, a feminine voice will ask for your "Number, please." Suppose, for example, that you wish to get Bryant 7-4310. Remove your hat politely and speak that number into the mouthpiece. The operator will then say, "Rhinelander 5-4310." To which you reply, "*No*, operator —*Bryant* 7-4310." She then says, "I beg your pardon— Bryant 7-4310," to which you reply, "Yes, please." In a few minutes a voice at the other end of the line says, "Hello," to which you answer, "Is Miss Doe at home?" The voice then says, "Who?" You say, "Miss Doe, please—Miss Dorothy Doe." You then hear the following, "Wait a minute. Say, Charlie, is they anybody works around here by the name of Doe? There's a guy wants to talk to a Miss Doe. Here—you answer it." Another voice then says, "Hello." You reply "Hello." He says, "What do you want?" You reply, "I wish to speak to Miss Dorothy Doe." He says, "What department does she work in?" You reply, "Is this the residence of J. Franklin Doe, President of the First National Bank?" He says, "Wait a minute." You wait a minute. You

wait several. Another voice—a new voice says—"Hello."
You reply "Hello." He says, "Give me Stuyvesant 2-8864."
You say, "But I'm trying to get Miss Doe—Miss Dorothy
Doe." He says, "Who?" You say, "Is this the residence of—"
He says, "Naw—this is Goebel Brothers, Wholesale Grocers
—what number do you want?" You say, "Bryant 7-4310."
He says, "Well, this is Rhinelander 5-4310." You then hang
up the receiver and count twenty. The telephone bell then
rings, and inasmuch as you are the only person near the
phone you take up the receiver and say, "Hello." A female
voice, says, "Hello, dearie—don't you know who this is?"
You say, politely but firmly, "No." She says, "Guess!" You
guess "Mrs. Harry Truman." She says, "No. This is Ethel.
Is Walter there?" You reply, "Walter?" She says, "Ask him
to come to the phone, will you? He lives up-stairs over the
drug store. Just yell 'Walter' at the third door down the
hall. Tell him Ethel wants to speak to him—no, wait—tell
him it's Madge." Being a gentleman, you comply with the
lady's request. After bringing Walter to the phone, you
obligingly wait for some twenty minutes while he converses
with Ethel—no, Madge. When he has finished, you once
more enter the booth and tell the operator you want Bryant
7-4310. After a few minutes the operator says, "What number did you call?" You say patiently, "Bryant 7-4310." She
replies, "Bryant 7-4310 has been changed to Schuyler
3-6372." You ask for Schuyler 3-6372. Finally a woman's
voice says, "Yass." You say, "Is Miss Doe in?" She replies,
"Yass." You say, "May I speak to her?" She says, "Who?"
You reply, "You said Miss Doe was at home, didn't you?"
She replies, "Yass." You say, "Well, may I speak to her?"
The voice says, "Who?" You shout, "Miss Doe." The voice
says, "She ban out." You shriek, "Oh, go to hell!" and assum-
ing a graceful, easy position in the booth, you proceed to
tear the telephone from the wall. Later on in the day, when

you have two or three hours of spare time, you can telephone Miss Doe again and arrange for the evening's visit.

The custom of social "calls" between young men and young women is one of the prettiest of etiquette's older conventions, and one around which clusters a romantic group of delightful traditions. In this day and generation, what with horseless carriages, electric telephones and telegraphs, and dirigible gas bags, a great many of the older forms have been allowed to die out, greatly, I believe, to our discredit. "Speed, not manners," seems to be the motto of this century. I hope that there still exist a few young men who care enough about "good form" to study carefully to perfect themselves in the art of "calling." Come, Tom, Dick and Harry—drop your bicycles for an afternoon and fill your minds with something besides steam engines and pneumatic tires!

The first call at the home of any young lady of fashion is an extremely important social function, and too great care can not be taken that you prepare yourself thoroughly in advance. It would be well to leave your work an hour or two earlier in the afternoon, so that you can go home and practice such necessary things as entering or leaving a room correctly. Most young men are extremely careless in this particular, and unless you rehearse yourself thoroughly in the proper procedure you are apt to find later on to your dismay that you have made your exit through a window onto the fire-escape instead of through the proper door.

CONVERSATION AND SOME OF ITS USES

Your conversation should also be planned more or less in advance. Select some topic in which you think your lady friend will be interested, such as, for example, the removal

of tonsils and adenoids, and "read up" on the subject so
that you can discuss it in an intelligent manner. Find out,
for example, how many people had tonsils removed in February, March, April. Contrast this with the same figures for
1880, 1890, 1900. Learn two or three amusing anecdotes
about adenoids. Consult Bartlett's "Familiar Quotations"
for appropriate verses dealing with tonsils and throat
troubles. Finally, and above all, take time to glance through
four or five volumes of Dr. Eliot's Five Foot Shelf, for nothing so completely marks the cultivated man as the ability
to refer familiarly to the various volumes of the Harvard
classics.

A PROPER CALL

Promptly at the time appointed you should arrive at
the house where the young lady is staying. In answer to
your ring a German police dog will begin to bark furiously
inside the house, and a maid will finally come to the door.
Removing your hat and one glove, you say, "Is Miss Doe
home?" The maid replies, "Yass, ay tank so." You give her
your card and the dog rushes out and bites you on either
the right or left leg. You are then ushered into a room in
which is seated an old man with a long white beard. He is
fast asleep. "Dot's grampaw," says the maid, to which you
reply, "Oh." She retires, leaving you alone with grampaw.
After a while he opens his eyes and stares at you for a few
minutes. He then says, "Did the dog bite you?" You answer,
"Yes, sir." Grampaw then says, "He bites everybody," and
goes back to sleep. Reassured, you light a cigaret. A little
boy and girl then come to the door, and, after examining
you carefully for several minutes, they burst into giggling
laughter and run away. You feel to see if you have forgotten
to put on a necktie. A severe looking old lady then enters
the room. You rise and bow. "I am Miss Doe's grandmother.
Some one has been smoking in here," she says, and sits

down opposite you. Her remark is not, however, a hint for a cigaret and you should not make the mistake of saying, "I've only got Parliaments, but if you care to try one—" It should be your aim to seek to impress yourself favorably upon every member of the young lady's family. Try to engage the grandmother in conversation, taking care to select subjects in which you feel she would be interested. Conversation is largely the art of "playing up" to the other person's favorite subject. In this particular case, for example, it would be a mistake to say to Miss Doe's grandmother, "Do you ever get lit on Saturday nights?" or "Do you think those wrestling matches on TV are phony?" A more experienced person, and some one who had studied the hobbies of old people, would probably begin by remarking, "Well, I see that Jeremiah Smith died of cancer Thursday," or "That was a lovely burial they gave Mrs. Watts, wasn't it?" If you are tactful, you should soon win the old lady's favor completely, so that before long she will tell you all about her rheumatism and what grampaw can and can't eat.

Finally Miss Doe arrives. Her first words are, "Have you been waiting long? Hilda didn't tell me you were here," to which you reply, "No—I just arrived." She then says, "Shall we go in the drawing-room?" The answer to this is, "For God's sake, yes!" In a few minutes you find yourself alone in the drawing-room with the lady of your choice and the courtship proper can then begin.

The best way to proceed is gradually to bring the conversation around to the subject of the "modern girl." After your preliminary remarks about tonsils and adenoids have been thoroughly exhausted, you should suddenly say, "Well, I don't think girls—nice girls—are really that way." She replies, of course, "*What* way?" You answer, "Oh, the way they are in these novels. This 'necking,' for instance." She says, "*What* 'necking?'" You walk over and sit down on the sofa beside her. "Oh," you say, "these novelists make me sick—they seem to think that every time a young man and woman are left alone together, they haven't a thing better to do than put out the light and 'neck.' It's disgusting, isn't it?" "Isn't it?" she agrees and reaching over she accidentally pulls the lamp cord, which puts out the light.

On your first visit you should not stay after 12:30.

THE PROPOSAL PROPER

About the second or third month of a formal courtship it is customary for the man to propose matrimony, and if the girl has been "out" for three or four years and has several younger sisters coming along, it is customary for her to accept him. They then become "engaged," and the courtship is concluded.

CONFETTI ON THE BRAIN

by Billy Rose

Some years ago, Billy Rose hired a young performer named Danny Kaye as a sort of assistant comic in one of his shows. Did Rose, one of the great showmen of our time, recognize Kaye's superior talents and elevate him to stardom? On the contrary, he confined him to an unimportant bit in the show.

Here is Billy Rose's sparkling and self-kidding dissertation on the discoveries he has missed, and on the formulas for success in show business.

ALL THIS stuff about my being an expert at picking pretty girls is so much smoke from a press agent's pipe. And the same goes for Sam Goldwyn and the late Earl Carroll. Anybody who can cross the street without a Seeing-Eye dog can pick a pretty girl.

When it comes to judging beauty, the wolf whistle is much more important than the tape measure. The experts tell you that a girl should have a 24 waist, 34 hips, and 34 you-know-whats. Arkus-malarkus! If she gives you goose bumps, hire her.

The key to collecting cuties is the same as the key to so many other problems—money! What you're willing to pay is ninety-nine percent of it. The other one percent is an eye sharp enough to read the top line on an optician's chart.

Let's see how Ziegfeld, the all-time boss of the beauty business, used to go about getting his girls. When the Equity minimum for show girls was thirty dollars a week, Ziggy was paying Gladys Glad and Lillian Lorraine as much as three hundred. When his competitors were spending sixty dollars on a girl's costume, the Great Glorifier was dolling them up in a thousand dollars' worth of beads and baubles.

No one ever scared off a honey by offering her clothes and money. Soon every girl with straight legs, straight nose and carfare headed for Ziggy's office. When the Great Man issued a chorus call, they had to summon the riot squad to keep the babes from taking his building apart. His competitors, paying a fast thirty a week, had to content themselves with seconds, thirds and twelfths.

A few years back I put on a revue called *Seven Lively Arts*. There was plenty of disagreement on the show's merits but none on the showgirls. People kept asking me where I got them. I winked and played genius.

Let me 'fess up. After several disappointing chorus calls, I dropped in to see Harry Conover, the model agent. I told him I was willing to pay a hundred a week for real sight-catchers. The next day his magazine-cover girls mobbed me. Herbert Hoover could have taken it from there.

What did I look for as they paraded around the stage? The same things you look for when you're standing on a windy corner.

Picking actresses, of course, is something else again. An interesting chest and a mess of grapefruit-colored hair aren't enough. If I were a theatrical agent trying to build up a stable of actresses to support me in my old age, I'd look

for two things in the girls who applied—(1) talent, and
(2) toughness.

By toughness I don't mean talking like a top sergeant
and forgetting what Mommy said about strange men. That
kind of toughness winds up in a beanery dealing them off
the arm, or down in South America pleasuring the coffee-
planters.

The kind of toughness I'm talking about is compounded
of ego, energy, and a white flame in the vitals. It's the kind
of toughness that makes a gal sing her head off on a
three-dollar club date at Botchi Galoopo's Bar and Grill.
It's the kind of toughness that shrugs off walking to
save carfare, sorry-you're-not-the-type-leave-your-name-
and-address, and the other assorted kicks in the slats.

A couple of centuries ago the babe who had this combination of talent and toughness was the person to see when you
wanted a favor from the King. In our time, she gets to be
an actress, a playwright, an editor, a designer, a Congress-
woman.

I hardly know Joan Crawford, but I've been watching
her ever since she did the Charleston in a nightclub across
the street from mine, back in the jazz-and-juniper days. I
saw her go to Hollywood, scratch her way to stardom, do
a fadeout when talkies came, learn how to act with words,
and then storm back to the top over mountains of younger
flesh. That's a toughie for you.

It was only a few years ago that I was paying Betty Hutton sixty bucks a week for kiyoodling with Vincent Lopez's
band at one of my cabarets. I've enjoyed seeing this baby-
face bite, kick, and somersault into an eminence which not
long ago commanded $28,000 for seven days at a Boston
theatre. Another pistol-packer.

I once bit chunks out of an orchestra seat while Tallulah
Bankhead held up a dress rehearsal to make sure she was

lighted properly. While stagehands played pinochle and the company went out for coffee, Tallulah made certain no unflattering shadow would hurt her appearance. The rehearsal cost me a lot of dough, but I couldn't help admiring this Humphrey Bogart in lace panties.

When I call these girls tough, I mean tough in the way a great fighter is tough. Not mean, not dirty—but slick, strong, smooth, and determined to be champ. Unless a gal has that kind of toughness to go with her talent, I think she'd better stay home, marry the butcher's son, and live in luxury forever after.

In addition to being talented and tough, it also helps if you're a bit of a screwball. A lot of people want to go on the stage. If you're one of them, I suggest you ask yourself seven questions before you leave home:

1. Are you normal? If you are, I don't think you've got much chance. What do you do in a thunderstorm—duck under a tree? Well, then, you're wrong for show business. An actor, when he hears thunder, stands there and takes bows.

2. Are you truthful? If you are, join the Boy Scouts. A trouper lies like a trouper—it's the nature of the animal. If an audience snickers, he tells you he fractured 'em. If an audience laughs, he'll tell you they had to be carried out on stretchers. The lowest gross in show business was chalked up a few years ago in Pittsburgh during a flood. By actual count the box office took in $6. The star of the show told the story this way: "We played to the smallest gross in history —$7."

3. Are you modest? Well, then, work in a coal mine. Do you walk into a room like people, or must it always be a Big Entrance? Wallace Reid, the silent-picture star, came late to the Dempsey-Carpentier fight. Just as he walked in, Car-

pentier drove Dempsey to the ropes and thirty acres of spectators went crazy. Reid bowed, turned to a friend, and said, "Isn't that nice of them?"

4. Are you reasonable? When you miss a short putt, do you blame yourself or some other fellow? Willie Collier was in a show that opened Thursday and folded Saturday. His comment was: "The play was a success, but the audience was a failure." Marlene Dietrich once complained to a photographer that his pictures of her weren't as glamorous as those he had taken some years back. The tactful cameraman replied, "You must remember, Miss Dietrich, I was eight years younger then."

5. Are you humble? Can you walk out on a stage, face a thousand strangers, and say with your eyes, "I'm wonderful. Love me!" Do you think you'd make a superb King Lear because you once made offstage noises in a high-school drama? Can you live up to the traditions of the actor on the ocean liner who fell overboard one stormy night? The ship stopped and its searchlight picked him out in the water. As he was going down for the third time, the hambo shouted, "Make that an amber spotlight!"

6. Are you romantic? Are you prepared to swap the cottage with the roses for the trunk with the stickers? Would you trade your girl for an electric sign? Do you prefer billing or cooing? If you hesitated for a moment on *this* question, don't bother answering.

7. Do you know when it's time to quit? If you do, I don't see much future for you. You've got to have the instincts of the fellow who gave up acting to become a surgeon. He removed an appendix so skillfully that the doctors watching him started to applaud. Whereupon he bowed and cut out the man's gall bladder for an encore.

If your answers to these seven questions indicate that you're wacky, a big fibber, swell-headed, bull-headed and fat-headed, then come to Broadway. There are about five hundred jobs available each season. You can be one of the ten thousand trying to get them.

One other thing before you start packing. Do you realize you're going up against a business in which good looks plus talent doesn't necessarily equal employment? Has anybody told you that most of the fellows who do the hiring on Broadway are dopes? Well, most of them are.

Take me for instance. My press agent is forever sending out stories about the stars I've discovered. Malarkey! When it comes to sitting down in a noisy rehearsal room and picking the star of tomorrow from fifty shaky youngsters, I'm as blind as Justice. As for instance:

Metro owns a couple of stars named Van Johnson and Esther Williams. Esther swam for me in the Aquacade at the Golden Gate Exposition. Van was a chorus boy at one of my cabarets in New York. Did I foresee that Van Johnson and Esther Williams would become two of the most valuable entertainment properties in the world? All together now—*in a pig's eye!*

When I was auditioning acts in Fort Worth in 1936, a girl warbled a chorus of an unhappy song called "Gloomy Sunday." I advised her to get married and tend to her dishes and diapers. A few years later a lovely in a Mainbocher gown came up to my table at the Stork Club and kissed me on top of my head. Sure, it was the same girl—Mary Martin —the biggest hunk of musical comedy talent since Gertie Lawrence came over from London with *Charlot's Revue,* in 1924.

Danny Kaye worked for me a few years ago. He stooged for a hoofer named Nick Long, Jr. I paid Danny $75 a week and permitted him to say exactly three words—"Soft and mellow." Betty Hutton worked at the same cabaret. While the trumpet player rested his lip, I used to let her sing a chorus with the band.

Where was Joe McGenius when all this talent was jiggling around his joints? Why didn't I sign these hot kids to long-term contracts? Well, I guess I was too busy reading the scrapbooks where it says I'm a smart showman.

A succession of press agents have claimed I gave Benny Goodman his start. Don't believe it. It's true I gave his band its first job at the Billy Rose Music Hall, but it only filled in while the other band was catching a smoke in the alley. When the whole country went crazy about B. G. and his Cats, I took a few bows here and there, but I never knew what all the hollering was about.

Louis Prima, the Andrews Sisters, Vera Allen, Abbott and Costello, Virginia Mayo, they all did bits in my shows before anybody realized they were anybody. I used them and forgot about them until their names exploded all over twenty thousand marquees.

Which all adds up to this: If you come to Broadway and have a tough time getting started, don't jump on a train— or in front of one. The producer who turns you down may be as big a dope as I am.

A few hundred words back I said there were only about 500 acting jobs each season. I wasn't kidding. We aren't producing as many shows as we used to. We can't afford to. Twenty years back, you could ring up the curtain on a legitimate show for $10,000. Today the same show costs $60,000. And when it comes to mounting a musical, its plain astronomy.

Recently I turned down the chance to produce a tune-and-tinsel frolic which had all the earmarks of a hit. A minute with a pencil showed it would cost over $200,000 to put it on. The show would have to gross better than

$25,000 a week to cover operating expenses. I decided not to do it, and have a good season.

What makes these cardboard-and-rhinestone *Schauspiels* cost so much? Why should a stage kitchen cost more than a home in Long Island with real plumbing? Why does an obscure hoofer who's on stage twenty-four minutes a week earn more than a fine painter like Thomas Benton?

Well, to begin with, show business isn't a business. It's a crap game. And there are no small salaries around a gambling house.

The showgirl costume that cost me a hundred bucks a few years ago now costs five hundred. Scenery, props, electrical equipment—you'd think they came from Tiffany's. The average teamster, stagehand, or musician earns more than a lot of our big-league ball players.

The economics of producing are so daffy these days that a show can run a year and lose a bundle. For instance, was *Showboat* a good show? Try to think of a better one. It grossed more than two million when it was revived at my theatre. Yet it wound up $160,000 in the red.

Another thing that makes producing a treacherous business these days is the thousand tired people who attend the opening night of a Broadway show.

For a lot of years now, I've been one of that thousand. The same bunch of us show up first night after first night in our penguin suits. We've eaten too much and generally have a few brandies under our belts. Another show to us is like another book to a librarian. It's my guess that not more than a hundred of us give a damn about the play.

Let's look at a typical opening night audience as it files into the theatre. First in their seats are the four people who don't consider themselves celebrities. Next come the relatives of the cast. Their prolonged applause for a bit player will again prove that blood is thicker than billing.

Taking their seats now are the actresses who read for the part but didn't get it. It's all right with them if the chosen one trips on her gown and falls into the orchestra pit. The closer her acting gets to Bernhardt, the closer they'll get to heartburn.

For every girl who didn't land the part there's an agent who didn't land the commission. He comes disguised as a human being, and he'll hate the play only ten percent as much as his client.

The theatre is beginning to fill up. Here come the set designers who didn't get to do the show. The only time they ever noticed the actors was the night *Our Town* was presented on a bare stage.

In the aisle seats you can pick out the critics. They usually eat a light dinner so as to leave room for the playwright.

Scattered through the audience are talent scouts from the gold-plated popcorn machine called Hollywood. These gents are merely killing time until intermission, when they will rush backstage and disrupt the company by offering some actor ten times as much as he is worth.

Down front are the rival producers, who look at the other fellow's play like a crocodile watches Tarzan trying to swing over a stream. As they come in, they wish the producer luck, the liars. The producer manages a tired quip: "What have I got to lose—only a lousy fortune!"

The author stands at the back, stabbing latecomers with his eyes. He wishes he had a machine gun as he watches them trample all over the first half-hour of something that represents a year's work.

By the time everyone is seated, the first act is over. The entire audience tries to crowd into a lobby hardly big enough for Sidney Greenstreet. The wits and clamor girls take over:

"I've had a lovely evening, but this isn't it."

"If anyone in the audience had a fish, what was he waiting for?"

"She's been playing ingenue parts since 34th Street was uptown."

A buzzer announces the second act. They stamp out their cigarettes and go in, having ruined the carpet and a dozen reputations.

About seventy-five shows open each season. Perhaps a baker's dozen successfully run the first-night gantlet. Every producer wishes he could unveil his show to the public and sidestep these cats-and-yammer kids. But I'm afraid there won't be any change in this setup until some inspired fellow figures out a way to open a show on the second night.

Of course I realize that the rusty harpoons I'm throwing at the legitimate theatre aren't going to stop anybody who really has what it takes. As long as one Barbara Bel Geddes can happen, a thousand would-be Barbaras are going to keep punching. They know that the payoff for the few who make good in the theatre is a fantastic one, not only in money but in prestige.

For reasons that are two thousand years old, the theatre has what the movies have never been able to buy—manners and tradition. The boys in the Beverly Hills bungalows may not like this, but to the acting profession, Hollywood is still the awkward newcomer to the show-business banquet—red-faced, bumbling, and waving money bags to hide its embarrassment. The performer knows that the runaway tailors on the West Coast haven't produced a writer in thirty years fit to shine the shoes of Sean O'Casey of the little Abbey Theatre in Dublin.

For years I've been listening to Hollywood actors cuss out the flicker factories which keep them in cookies and convertibles. For years I've watched $2,000-a-week script writers pant for a chance to get back to Shubert Alley with that play they've been writing on M-G-M's time.

I know what is biting them. Like everybody else, they yen to be involved in classy goings-on, and no matter how much Louis B. Mayer pays them, he'll never get it out of their heads that the theatre is the Rembrandt of show business. . . .

I'd like to wind up this chapter by telling you a little story. If you have a record of Irving Berlin's "There's No Business Like Show Business," it might be a nice touch to play it as background music.

When I got into trouble with my first musical back in 1931, I decided to kiss the theatre goodbye. Late one night at the old Friars Club, I told George M. Cohan what I had decided. The Yankee Doodle kid said, "I don't blame you, Billy. I think you've made a smart decision.

"Your hard luck this season reminds me of another hard-luck showman I happen to know of. When he took out his first show—and it wasn't much of a show by our standards —he was twenty-six years old.

"His first stop was a small town in Massachusetts. The hotel in which his troupe was staying caught fire that night and some of his costumes were burned. Then at the next stop, a hell-fire-and-brimstone parson ran him out of town.

"A bit discouraged, he headed south. In Roanoke, Virginia, it rained so hard he had to cancel his show. The owner of the hotel where the performers were to have stayed threatened to have the producer jailed unless he paid for the three meals and lodging which had been arranged for. The producer paid up—but only after his company ate the three meals at one sitting and lay down on the beds for half an hour to soil the sheets.

"In South Carolina, his star colored singer walked out. The producer rubbed some burnt cork on his face and did the fellow's numbers himself. As he came off, he heard an argument between his ticket taker and one of the natives. The producer, still blacked up, butted in and talked tough.

"The Carolinian whipped out a pistol. No colored man was going to get uppity with him. The producer had to roll up his sleeves and show his white skin to keep from getting shot.

"One night the magician's assistant didn't show up. The producer crawled into the trick compartment under the table and handed up the props which the magician was supposedly producing out of thin air. One of these props was a live squirrel. It bit the producer in the soft part of the back. He leaped out of the compartment and ran ki-yi-ing through the audience. The crowd threatened to break up his show and he had to give their money back.

"Down in Mississippi he picked up a showboat—not the one they sing about, but a beat-up hulk which would have turned over if fifteen people leaned against the same rail. The second day out, one of his minstrels fell over the side and drowned.

"For the next few weeks, whenever the producer ran short of cash he would sell a piece of his show. I don't mean a financial interest—no one would buy that. I mean a curtain, an old trunk, or one of his musicians' instruments.

"By the time he got to New Orleans, there wasn't much left of the show. He traded what remained for a few kegs of blackstrap molasses.

"The producer swore he would never mess with show business again. And he didn't—until the following season.

"Unlike you, my dear Billy, P. T. Barnum didn't know enough to quit when the quitting was good."

MADAME DU BARRY

by Will Cuppy

Our next selection is a full account, complete with Will Cuppy's famous footnotes, of the romance of King Louis XV and Jeanne du Barry. Mr. Cuppy, in his sly and meticulous way, never misses a detail, from the cups of coffee Jeanne used to brew, to the matter of a certain Miss Murphy (see footnote 8). All we can say is that our history lessons at school were never like this.

It's easy, of course, to see the reason King Louis was attracted to Madame du Barry. After all, there's nothing like a good— but why spoil the punch line?

JEANNE DU BARRY was a dear friend of Louis XV for about six years, from 1768 until his death in 1774. At first glance this would seem to be nobody's business, except possibly Jeanne's and Louis's, yet it is part of history and should be written up every so often to show how foolish people were in those days. They believed we were put here to have a good time.

Jeanne was the daughter of Anne Bécu, a seamstress of considerable industry and skill. Anyhow, she owned a couple of fur coats. In the way of business she met one Jean-Baptiste Gomard, who proved to be like all the men, and Little Jeanne was born on August 19, 1743. This made the baby a Leo character with a mere touch of Virgo.[1]

As a young girl Jeanne was no loafer. She tried several jobs as companion or domestic but had trouble in holding them. She was always getting thrown out on her ear by the lady of the house. Since she was poor, she had never been taught to behave properly, the way the upper classes behave.[2] And we really shouldn't blame her for having ash-blonde curls, enormous blue eyes, and a perfect disposition.

Sometimes the going was rather lively. When she was fifteen, a young hairdresser spent so much time teaching her the tricks of the trade that his mother raised a row, calling Jeanne's mother some dreadful names. Anne Bécu took the woman to court on a charge of slander, and the judge advised her to drop it. Police records do not support the story that Jeanne also worked for Madame Gourdan, the worst old lady in Paris. The fellow who started it after Jeanne had become a success said he had seen her at Madame Gourdan's with his own eyes. By the way, what was *he* doing there?

At seventeen Jeanne was employed at the Maison Labille, a millinery shop frequented by gay young blades and oglers of all ages.[3] One of her acquaintances at this period was Monsieur Duval, a clerk in the Marine,[4] whom she soon threw over for Monsieur Radix de Sainte-Foix, treasurer of the Marine.[5] Thenceforth Jeanne's deeper infatuations always seemed to concern gentlemen of a certain age and standing in the financial world. Older men say such inter-

---

[1] Anne could cook, too, and later followed that profession.

[2] For a time she attended an institution for young persons "who may find themselves in danger of being ruined." She stayed only one term.

[3] Ogling has been sadly neglected since the eighteenth century. Our modern life is so rushed—no poetry.

[4] You have to start somewhere.

[5] I say nothing of the Abbé de Bonnac. Why bring those things up?

esting things, and Jeanne was always a good listener. Anything you said was news to her.

She also met at this time the bogus Comte Jean du Barry, a roué who ran a gambling house for noblemen and wealthy citizens. I am afraid Jeanne moved into this establishment and stayed there several years. Even her detractors agree, however, that she was only a friend to the count, as he was not in the best of health, anyway. Among other things, he suffered from inflammation of the eyes and for this complaint generally wore two baked apples on the top of his head, holding them in place with his hat. I never heard how the treatment turned out.

Du Barry simply wanted Jeanne to dress up the place, meet his more important guests, and make them feel at home. She was the right girl for the job, being naturally kind and sympathetic. She couldn't bear to see an old millionaire off in a corner looking lonely and sad and always did her best to cheer such people up. In no time at all she learned exactly how to handle old gentlemen, an accomplishment which was to stand her in good stead before long. Meanwhile, she made some splendid connections.

One is not sure how Jeanne and Louis met. We only know that it was June, in 1768, that she was twenty-five and he was on the loose. June was wonderful that year. The Queen had died on the twenty-fourth.[6] Shortly before that, Louis had interviewed Jeanne, as he called it, and pretty soon she moved into an apartment at Versailles directly above his, to the horror of several duchesses who had hoped to occupy them and had pestered the life out of Louis since the passing of Madame de Pompadour in 1764. Pompadour had been with him for twenty years, a record for this reign.[7]

[6] Queen Marie Leszczinska had been at Versailles since 1725. For the last thirty years she just lived there.

[7] A lot of ideas can be exchanged in twenty years—in fact, all of them.

Pompadour's death had left his private life completely empty, with nobody in it but his wife and children.

Since then, of course, he had interviewed dozens of young women, including a Miss Smith, who did not click.[8] But he had not had an official mistress for the last four years, a state of affairs which could hardly be allowed to continue, you must admit.[9] Since Jeanne could not be presented at court without certain improvements in her social status, Louis married her off to Guillaume du Barry, a brother of Jean.[10] Although their title was spurious, the Du Barrys were gentlemen, since none of their ancestors had ever done an honest day's work as far back as the records went. The marriage therefore made Jeanne a respectable woman so that she could associate with Louis in public or private or both.

Thus Jeanne became Madame du Barry and took her place in history. Guillaume left town with Madeleine Lemoine, and everything was fine except for the disappointed ladies and a few others whose morals couldn't face it. Many people believed then, as they do today, that it is more immoral to have a lowborn mistress. It isn't, really.[11] The Duchesse de Gramont, who had been trying to make Louis, was fit to be tied, and Marie Antoinette, who came to Versailles as the wife of Louis's grandson, the Dauphin, was shocked at the mere thought. Marie Antoinette's mate, the future Louis XVI, was quite different from his grandfather

[8] And a Miss Murphy, who did.

[9] The technical term for this position was *maîtresse déclarée*, or *maîtresse en titre*. Today we wouldn't bother to name it.

[10] The surname De Vaubernier under which Jeanne is often catalogued in libraries appeared first in her wedding papers. It's a phony.

[11] There was some raising of eyebrows—unjustified, it seems to me—at the Du Barry coat of arms, which contained as its motto the perfectly good old war cry, *"Boutez en Avant!"* or "Push Forward!"

in some respects, and she had plenty of time to gossip.[12] An anti-Du Barry party grew up at court, and quite a number of courtiers never forgave either of the happy pair.

Some historians have wondered why Louis XV would take up with a young person of Jeanne's humble origin when he could have had one of those horse-faced duchesses with correct manners. One reason was that Louis, although he was fifty-eight, still had his eyesight. In an effort to clarify the whole situation and stop the arguments about why he did it, Louis wrote to his chief minister, the Duc de Choiseul, "She is very pretty, she pleases me, and that should be enough." This statement completely baffled everybody who read it or heard it.[13]

Louis's general outlook was, to be candid, extremely limited. He was a one-idea man. He believed that what is worth doing at all is worth doing as often as is humanly possible. He had been at it for forty years, off and on, and he wondered why he saw spots. You're going to say that he should have worked up an interest in the birds and the flowers. He did try. He kept some cages of birds in a back room, together with a few books, some old maps, and a huge collection of assorted candy. For a while he studied botany in the gardens of Versailles. But it wasn't the same thing, somehow.[14]

And so there were great days and nights in Jeanne's apartments at the top of the stairs, one flight up. In my opinion, however, the sinful nature of these sessions has been exaggerated. No doubt Louis had been quite a fellow in his time, but his conversational powers had begun to

---

[12] Marie Antoinette wrote to her brother, later the Emperor Joseph II of Austria, "My husband is a poor fish." That seems to cover it.

[13] You can always win a Ph.D. in history by trying to interpret that statement in all its aspects and ramifications. No two Ph.D.'s agree on its meaning.

[14] He once sent strawberry seeds to Linnaeus. And why not?

wane and it was common gossip that his celery tonic didn't help much any more.[15] Perhaps the truth is that Louis could relax when he was with Jeanne. I doubt if he even tried to live up to his reputation as a great big brute.

Jeanne was always lively and gay, and Louis loved gaiety, though his own attempts in that line had never been too successful. In an effort to be a good fellow he once stomped on the foot of a courtier suffering gout, but nobody laughed and he retired from the field of wit and humor.[16] Jeanne was jolly enough for both. She would throw a box of powder in his face and call him John the Miller and he would roar with laughter. Or she would use highly unconventional words in casual conversation, whereat he would all but split his sides. Well, that sort of thing can be very funny.

There was the coffee, too. No doubt you have heard how Louis would prepare it himself in Jeanne's small kitchen, how she would jest when it boiled over, and how they would drink it together in those pleasant rooms. Louis became more addicted to the beverage with the years, and things were so arranged that he could have a cup at any hour of the day or night if he felt the urge. His doctor warned him against the habit, for Louis began to have dizzy spells after he reached his sixties. It wasn't the coffee. It was those damned stairs.

What, aside from her beauty and her merry spirit, was the secret of Du Barry's charm? How did she manage to hold her aging varietist—much the worst kind—until the end, in the face of scandal, intrigue, and good-looking

[15] The Countess d'Esparbes told one of her cronies that Louis had taken a dose of his tonic before interviewing her in 1764, quite without effect. Louis banished her from court, and served her right.

[16] The fellow left Versailles in a rage and could never be induced to return. It takes two to make a joke.

strangers, and even keep him fairly true to her? [17] The
answer is that she let him alone sometimes. If he wanted
an afternoon off to make a snuffbox, that was all right with
her.[18] If he said he might be kept late at the office, she told
him to have a good time and she'd be seeing him. She did
not tell him that she had given him the best years of her
life and she supposed she could sit there alone all evening
long and who cared and why should anyone ever give her
a single thought. That's just my guess.

I suppose I must mention Jeanne's passion for clothes
and jewels. There was that, yet is it fair to assume that she
loved Louis for his money? Be that as it may, she bought
new dresses and new diamonds every day, and she could
have the place done over as often as she wished without
a squawk from headquarters. Louis was the soul of gener-
osity, and that's something in a man, isn't it? He never
hesitated an instant to spend a million or two of the State
funds on her whims, even when business conditions were
awful.[19]

After a while Louis let her draw her own drafts on the
comptroller-general. It saved time and bother in a field he
much disliked.[20] Jeanne never took more than she needed
for urgent current expenses—that is, whatever was in the
treasury. According to one estimate, she accounted for
something like $62,409,015 in five years and, naturally, any
lady would feel deep gratitude for such a sum. Whether that
amount of money will purchase real, honest-to-God love,

[17] Which is more than Madame de Pompadour could do, and Pompadour had brains.

[18] She was probably tickled pink.

[19] The only thing he ever refused her was a solid gold toilet set,
and that was because a meddling official was making cracks about
extravagance at court. Jeanne had to cancel the order and get along
with silver until it blew over.

[20] The mere mention of finance made Louis XV ill. I'm the same
way myself.

though, I don't know. They say not, and I guess it's pretty low even to raise the question.

Well, nothing lasts forever, you know. Louis XV died of smallpox in May, 1774. Five days before the end he sent Jeanne away to prove that he was truly repentant. He had stood by her through thick and thin and only dismissed her for fear he would go to the bad place if he didn't. He loved her, but he balked at that. Had he recovered, he would almost certainly have brought her back. At least, let us hope so. Certain duchesses were delighted, and Marie Antoinette wrote to her mother, Maria Theresa, "The creature has been put in a convent, and everyone whose name was associated with the scandal has been driven from court."

When his funeral procession passed, nobody cried, "Here comes Louis the Well-Beloved!" as the mob had done many years before, after his illness at Metz, when they believed he had won a war practically singlehanded and worn himself out for their sake. He had only made himself sick carousing with the Duchesse de Chateauroux, but they didn't know that. Now hecklers laughed at the hearse and shouted, "There goes the Ladies' Delight!" That's more than you can say of *some* people.[21]

Jeanne lived on for almost twenty years, rich, active in good works, not without a few sweethearts, a little plumper but still pretty as a picture at fifty. She was one of the victims of the French Revolution, a thing thought up by some philosophers who wished to make the world a better place to live in. They wanted all the French to be free and equal and happy, and they tried to bring this about by decapitating as many of them as possible. Jeanne went to the guillotine for her royalist sympathies in 1793.[22] The

[21] They were not moral bigots. They were sore about the taxes.
[22] Marie Antoinette's turn had come just two months earlier.

charge was true enough. Jeanne did not like the common people. She knew them too well.[23]

Nothing could be more erroneous than the widespread notion that Madame du Barry caused the French Revolution. That was the last thing she had on her mind. She only wanted bushels of beautiful money to spend on fripperies. She had harmed nobody in the days of her glory, unless it was the Duc de Choiseul, who crossed her once too often about the bank account. She had him fired and made Louis pay him a staggering pension so that the poor man wouldn't mind too much.[24] She was the last left-hand Queen of France.

I never dwell upon that scene at the guillotine when I think of Madame du Barry. I prefer to see her in her proper setting at Versailles, in the little apartment one flight up and walk right in. One sees Louis, too, puffing up the back stairs at midnight in the royal shirttail, slightly purple in the face, fairly bursting with anticipation and arteriosclerosis. He opens the door and there is Jeanne in a fetching negligee, looking more like an angel than ever. Well, there's nothing like a good cup of coffee.

[23] Jean du Barry, the roué, was decapitated for being a gentleman, if only on paper. Guillaume, Jeanne's legal husband, beat the rap and married Madeleine.

[24] Choiseul was always mean to Du Barry, fearing that she would try to run the country. Jeanne knew nothing about the silly old country and cared less. She only wanted her own way.

MONEY

by Richard Armour

Workers earn it,
Spendthrifts burn it,
Bankers lend it,
Women spend it,
Forgers fake it,
Taxes take it,
Dying leave it,
Heirs receive it,
Thrifty save it,
Misers crave it,
Robbers seize it,
Rich increase it,
Gamblers lose it . . .
I could use it.

HERR OTTO BRAUHAUS

by Ludwig Bemelmans

Ludwig Bemelmans was a hotel employee in various capacities before he turned to writing, and many of his stories and articles are based on his experiences in this field. The selection that follows is one of them, as warm and amusing a pen portrait as we've read in a long time.

Bemelmans is also a successful artist, and does many magazine covers and illustrations for his own stories. A long-time sufferer from insomnia, he does much of his work in the wee hours.

THE SPLENDIDE had four hundred rooms, a great number for a luxurious hotel. Hotels larger than this become like railroad stations, eating and sleeping institutions. They have to take in anyone who comes along. The staff changes too frequently to give perfect service, to become acquainted with the guests. In the bigger hotels, the manager is usually a financial person, a one-time accountant who leaves actual contact with the guests to a platoon of day and night assistants, a kind of floorwalker with a small desk in the middle of the lobby and no authority except to say good-morning and good-night, a man whose business it is to shake hands and watch the bellboys and be in charge in case of fire.

In a hotel like the Splendide, however, it must be assumed, for the purposes of good management, that every guest is a distinguished and elegant person who, of course, has a great deal of money. The prices are high and must be high; the cost of provisions is probably the smallest item. The charges are for marble columns, uniforms, thick carpets, fine linen, thin glasses, many servants, and a good orchestra. And the management of such a hotel is a difficult, delicate business. It produces in most cases a type of man whose face is like a towel on which everyone has wiped his hands, a smooth, smiling, bowing man, in ever freshly pressed clothes, a flower in his lapel, précieux and well fed.

Rarely does one find in America a hotel manager who has survived the winds of complaint, the climate of worry, and the floods of people, and of whom one can still say that, besides being short or tall, thin or fat, he has this or that kind of a personality. Such a one, a real person, honest, always himself with a unique character, was Otto Brauhaus, manager of the Hotel Splendide.

Otto Brauhaus was an immense stout man; he had to bend down to pass under the tall doorways of his hotel. Big as his feet, which gave him much trouble, telegraphing their sorrows to his ever-worried face, was his heart. For despite his conception of himself as a stern executive, and strict disciplinarian, he could not conceal his kindness. He liked to laugh with guests and employees alike, and the result was that his countenance was the scene of an unending emotional conflict.

He was a German, from the soft-speaking Palatinate. For all his years in America, he had somehow never been able to improve his accent. Too genuine a person to learn the affected English of Monsieur Victor, who was a fellow-countryman, Brauhaus spoke a thick dialect that sometimes sounded like a vaudeville comedian trying for effect. He

was, in any case, inarticulate, and hated to talk. Two ex-
pressions recurred in his speech like commas; without them
he seemed hardly able to speak: "Cheeses Greisd!" and
"Gotdemn it!"

His friends were all solid men like himself. Most of them
seemed to be brewers, and they would have occasional din-
ners together, small beer-fests, up in the top-floor suite.
There they drank enormous quantities of beer and ate canvasback ducks with wild rice. They held little speeches
afterwards and ate again at midnight. They spoke mostly
about how proud they were of being brewers. Almost weep-
ing with sentiment and pounding on the table with his fist,
one of them would always get up and say: "My father was
a brewer. So was my grandfather, and his father was a
brewer before him. I feel beer flowing in my veins."

Then Herr Brauhaus usually summed up their feelings
by rising to say: "My friends, we are all here together
around this table because we are friends. I am demn glad to
see all my friends here." They would all nod and applaud
and drink again.

But things had not been going too well with Brauhaus's
friends, these elderly men who ate and drank too well. In
one week Mr. Brauhaus went to two funerals. He came back
very gloomy from the second, saying: "Gotdemn it, Cheeses
Greisd, every time I see a friend of mine, he's dead."

Beautiful was it also when he described his art gallery.
Of the Rubens sketch he owned, he often said: "If something happens to me, Anna still has the Rubens," and of his
primitives he said: "Sometimes when I'm alone, I look at
them, and they look at me, so brimidif, like this," and he
would look sideways out of his face, just like his primitives.

He was not given to false conceptions of personal dignity though he insisted on his hotel's being treated with
proper respect. Once when he had hung up outside his of-

fice, one hour after he had bought it, a beautiful expensive heavy coat lined with mink, and it was stolen, Mr. Brauhaus ran out into the luncheon crowd which filled the lobby and howled: "Where is my furgoat, Cheeses Greisd!" But it was gone and never came back.

On the other hand one day when Mr. Brauhaus happened to be walking through the Jade Lounge, he saw an elderly lady sitting there alone at a small glasstop table, on which were tea and crumpets. She was knitting. Turning to me he said: "What do they think this is? Go over there and tell that woman to stop knitting." He pronounced the "k" in the last word. "Tell her that this is a first-class hotel and we don't want any knitting here in our Jade Lounges." He disappeared into his office.

I was a little afraid to follow orders, for the elderly lady was severely dressed and looked quite able of taking care of herself. I therefore passed the *patron's* instructions on to Monsieur Serafini, who looked at the lady, went "Tsk, tsk, tsk" with his tongue, and called a waiter. Fortunately, before the waiter could reach her, the old lady packed her knitting into an immense bag and smiled up at a tall man who had come in the door. She was his mother, and he was the new British Ambassador.

Brauhaus's goodness of heart, his reliance on the decency of his people, his unwillingness to face them when they had caused trouble, meant that he was always being taken advantage of by the smooth, tricky, much-traveled people who were his employees. "Why doesn't everybody do his duty, why do I have to bawl them out all the time?" he pleaded with them.

But when someone went too far, then Otto Brauhaus exploded. His big face turned red, his voice keeled over, he yelled and threatened murder. The culprit's head some-

where on a level with Brauhaus's watch chain, the storm
and thunder of the big man's wrath would tower and sweep
over him. Brauhaus's fists would be raised up at the ceiling,
pounding the air; the crystals on the chandelier would
dance at the sound of his voice: "I'll drow you oud, I'll kill
you, gotdemn it, Cheeses Greisd, ged oud of here!"

Fifteen minutes later, he enters his office and finds waiting for him the man he has been shouting at. Brauhaus
looks miserable, stares at the floor like a little boy. He puts
his hand on the man's shoulder and squeezes out a few embarrassed sentences. First he says: "Ah, ah—ah," then
comes a small prayer: "You know I am a very pusy man. I
have a lot of worries. I get excited and then I say things I
don't mean. You have been here a long time with me, and
I know you work very hard, and that you are a nice feller."
Finally a few more "Ah—ah—ah's," and then he turns
away. To any man with a spark of decency, all this hurts;
almost there are tears in one's eyes and one's loyalty to
Otto Brauhaus is sewn doubly strong with the big stitches
of affection.

Since he could not fire anyone, someone else had to get
rid of the altogether impossible people, and then an elaborate guard had to be thrown around Brauhaus to keep the
discharged employees from reaching him in person or by
telephone. Once a man got by this guard, all the firing was
for nothing.

One night it was announced that Mr. Brauhaus was
leaving on his vacation. Such information seeps through
the hotel immediately, as in a prison. The trunks were sent
on ahead, and late that night Mr. Brauhaus took a cab to
the station. But he missed his train, and, since the hotel was
not far from the station, he decided to walk back. With his
little Tirolese hat, his heavy cane, and his dachshund, which
he took with him on trips, he came marching into his hotel.

Outside he found no carriage man, no doorman, inside no one to turn the revolving door, no night clerk, also no bellboy and no elevator man. The lobby was quite deserted; only from the cashier's cage came happy voices and much laughter.

Mr. Brauhaus stormed back there and exploded: "What is diss? Gotdemn it! Cheeses Greisd! You have a birdtay zelepration here?"

They made themselves scarce and rushed for their posts. Only the bottles of beer were left, as the revolving door was turned, without guests in it, the elevator starter slipped on his gloves, and the night-clerk vaulted behind the counter and began to write. "You are fired, all fired, every-one here is fired, gotdemn it!" screamed Herr Brauhaus. "Everyone here is fired, you hear, *raus*, every one, you and you and you." He growled on: *"Lumpenpack, Tagediebe, Schweinebande!"* He had never heard or seen anything like this.

The men very slowly started to leave. "No, not now, come back, tomorrow you are fired," Brauhaus shouted at them.

He was so angry he could not think of going to sleep, and as always on the occasions when he was upset, he walked all the way around the hotel and back to the main en-trance. There the doorman got hold of him. With sad eyes, he intercepted Mr. Brauhaus, mumbled something about the twelve years he had been with the hotel, that only to-night, for the first time, had he failed in his duty, that he had a sick child and a little house in Flatbush and that his life would be ruined.

"All right," said Brauhaus. "You stay, John. All the others, gotdemn it, are fired."

But there was no one to protect him that night. Inside he heard the same story, with changes as to the particular family misfortunes and the location of the little houses.

They had all been with the Splendide since the hotel was built; the bellboy had gray hair and was fifty-six years old. Mr. Brauhaus walked out again and around the block. When he came back, he called them all together. He delivered them what was for him a long lecture on discipline, banging the floor with his stick, while the dachshund smelled the doorman's pants.

"I am a zdrikt disziblinarian," he said. They would all have to work together; this hotel was not a gotdemn joke, Cheeses Greisd. It was hard enough to manage it when everyone did his duty, gotdemn it. "And now get back to work."

A late guest arrived. He was swung through the door, saluted, wished a good-night, expressed up to his room with a morning paper and a passkey in the hands of the gray-haired bellboy. No guest had ever been so well and quickly served. "That's good, that's how it should be all the time," said Otto Brauhaus. "Why isn't it like this all the time?" Then he went to bed.

Besides all of Mr. Brauhaus's other troubles, there was the World War, and his hotel was filled in front with guests, and staffed in the rear with employees, of every warring nation. Whenever this problem arose, he always shouted: "We are all neudral here, gotdemn it, and friendts!"

One Thursday afternoon, about five-thirty, I had been sent to the kitchen to get some small sandwiches for some tea guests. The man who makes these sandwiches is called the *garde-manger*. Instead of ovens, this cook has only large iceboxes, in which he keeps caviar, pâté de foie gras, herrings, pickles, salmon, sturgeon, all the various hams, cold turkeys, partridges, tongues, the cold sauces, mayonnaise. Next to him is the oysterman, so that all the cold things are together.

In spite of being in a cool place instead of, as most cooks are all day, in front of a hot stove, this man was as nervous and excitable as any cook. Also I came at the worst possible time to ask anything of a cook, that is, while he was eating. He sat all the way in the back of his department, and before him were a plate of warm soup on a marble-topped table and a copy of the *Courrier des Etats Unis*, which announced in thick headlines a big French victory on the western front.

To order the sandwiches, the commis had first to write out a little slip, announce the order aloud, go to the coffee-man at the other end of the kitchen for the bread, and finally bring the bread to the garde-manger to be spread with butter, covered, and cut into little squares.

The garde-manger was still eating, but since the guest was in a hurry, I repeated the order to him. "Go away," the cook said angrily. "Can't you see I'm eating? Come back later."

I insisted he make the sandwiches now. "Go away!" he repeated. "*Sale Boche!*"

I called him a French pig. Near him was a box of little iceflakes to put under cold dishes; he reached into this box, came forward, and threw a handful of ice into my face. On the stone counter next to me stood a tower of heavy silver platters, oval, thick, and each large enough to hold six lobsters on ice; I took one of these platters, swung, and let it fly. It wabbled through the air, struck him at the side of the head between the eye and ear, and then fell on the tiled floor with a loud clatter. A woman who was scrubbing a table close by screamed.

Her scream brought the cooks from all the departments as well as the cooks who were eating—my old Frenchman of the fruit baskets and the first chef. Four of them carried the garde-manger to the open space in front of the ranges.

There he kicked and turned up his eyes; blood ran from the side of his face, and skin hung down under a wide gash. They poured water on him, shouted for the police, and everybody ran around in circles.

It was then I put into practice the Splendide maxim I had already learned: Get to Mr. Brauhaus first. I ran up the stairs and found him as usual worrying in his office under the sign: "Don't worry, it won't last, nothing does." I told him my story as quickly as I could. "What did he call you?" said Mr. Brauhaus, getting up. "A *Boche*, a *sale Boche?* Come with me." He took me by the hand and we went down to the kitchen.

On one side of the garde-manger stood all the cooks; on the other, the waiters, most of whom were Germans. But the French and the Italians waiters were also with them, for all waiters hate all cooks and all cooks hate all waiters. In the forefront of the waiters was Monsieur Victor; in the van of the cooks stood the first chef.

One side was dressed in white, the other in black. The cooks fiddled around in the air with knives and big ladles, and the waiters with napkins. They insulted each other and each other's countries; even the calm first chef was red in the face. The garde-manger lay on the floor, no longer kicking; sometimes he gulped and his lips fluttered. I thought he was going to die while we waited for an ambulance.

Everyone made room for Mr. Brauhaus. He waved them all back to work and went into the office with the first chef and me. "You hear me, Chef," he said, "I don't want no gotdemn badriodism in this gotdemn hotel, only good cooking and good service is what I want, Cheeses Greisd!" If the cook had done his work, he said, and not called me a *"sale Boche,"* he would not have had his head knocked in; he got what he deserved and he, Brauhaus, wasn't sorry for him. "This little poy is not to blame, it's your gotdemn dumm cooks," he shouted.

When the garde-manger came out of the hospital after some days, he waited for me on the service stairs of the hotel. "Hsst!" he said, and pointed to his head turbaned in bandages. "You know," he went on, "perhaps I should not have insulted you. I am sorry and here is my hand." I shook his hand. "But," he said, pointing again to his head, "it would be very dear for you, my friend, if I should make you pay for the pain. But let us forget that, I will ask you to pay only for the doctor and the hospital. Here is the bill, it is seventy-five dollars."

I did not have that much money, of course, but Monsieur Serafini lent it to me out of his pocket after I had signed a note promising to pay it back in weekly installments of five dollars.

GUINEA PIG

by Ruth McKenney

Whether she is writing about her sister, as she does in most of the stories in her famous *My Sister Eileen,* or about herself, as in the selection that follows, Ruth McKenney is magnificent. There are comparatively few first-line women humorists, but Miss McKenney evens the score by being as funny as six humorists all by herself.

"Guinea Pig" is the story of the time Miss McKenney tried to learn lifesaving, and of the curious way in which the Red Cross changed from angels of mercy into diabolical monsters out to drown her. As a noted philosopher once remarked, or should have remarked, the trouble with safety measures is that you can get killed learning them.

I WAS nearly drowned, in my youth, by a Red Cross Life-saving Examiner, and I once suffered, in the noble cause of saving human life from a watery grave, a black eye which was a perfect daisy and embarrassed me for days. Looking back on my agonies, I feel that none of my sacrifices, especially the black eye were in the least worth while. Indeed, to be brutally frank about it, I feel that the whole modern school of scientific lifesaving is a lot of hogwash.

Of course, I've had rather bad luck with lifesavers, right

from the beginning. Long before I ever had any dealings with professional lifesavers my sister nearly drowned me, quite by mistake. My father once took us to a northern Michigan fishing camp, where we found the life very dull. He used to go trolling for bass on our little lake all day long, and at night come home to our lodge, dead-beat and minus any bass. In the meantime Eileen and I, who were nine and ten at the time, used to take an old rowboat out to a shallow section of the lake and, sitting in the hot sun, feed worms to an unexciting variety of small, undernourished fish called gillies. We hated the whole business.

Father, however, loved to fish, even if he didn't catch a single fish in three weeks, which on this trip he didn't. One night, however, he carried his enthusiasm beyond a decent pitch. He decided to go bass fishing after dark, and rather than leave us alone in the lodge and up to God knows what, he ordered us to take our boat and row along after him.

Eileen and I were very bored rowing around in the dark, and finally, in desperation, we began to stand up and rock the boat, which resulted, at last, in my falling into the lake with a mighty splash.

When I came up, choking and mad as anything, Eileen saw me struggling, and, as she always says with a catch in her voice, she only meant to help me. Good intentions, however, are of little importance in a situation like that. For she grabbed an oar out of the lock, and with an uncertain gesture hit me square on the chin.

I went down with a howl of pain. Eileen, who could not see much in the darkness, was now really frightened. The cold water revived me after the blow and I came to the surface, considerably weakened but still able to swim over to the boat. Whereupon Eileen, in a noble attempt to give me the oar to grab, raised it once again, and socked me square on the top of the head. I went down again, this time without a murmur, and my last thought was a vague wonder that my own sister should want to murder me with a rowboat oar.

As for Eileen, she heard the dull impact of the oar on my head and saw the shadowy figure of her sister disappear. So she jumped in the lake, screeching furiously, and began to flail around in the water, howling for help and looking for me. At this point I came to the surface and swam over to the boat, with the intention of killing Eileen.

Father, rowing hard, arrived just in time to pull us both out of the water and prevent me from attacking Eileen with the rowboat anchor. The worst part about the whole thing, as far as I was concerned, was that Eileen was considered a heroine and Father told everybody in the lake community that she had saved my life. The postmaster put her name in for a medal.

After what I suffered from amateur lifesaving, I should have known enough to avoid even the merest contact with the professional variety of water mercy. I learned too late that being socked with an oar is as nothing compared to what the Red Cross can think up.

From the very beginning of that awful lifesaving course I took the last season I went to a girls' camp, I was a marked woman. The rest of the embryo lifesavers were little, slender maidens, but I am a peasant type, and I was monstrously big for my fourteen years. I approximated, in poundage anyway, the theoretical adult we energetic young lifesavers were scheduled to rescue, and so I was, for the teacher's purpose, the perfect guinea pig.

The first few days of the course were unpleasant for me, but not terribly dangerous. The elementary lifesaving hold, in case you haven't seen some hapless victim being rescued by our brave beach guardians, is a snakelike arrangement for supporting the drowning citizen with one hand while you paddle him in to shore with the other. You are supposed to wrap your arm around his neck and shoulders, and keep his head well above water by resting it on your collarbone.

This is all very well in theory, of course, but the trick that none of Miss Folgil's little pupils could master was keeping the victim's nose and mouth above the waterline. Time and again I was held in a viselike grip by one of the earnest students with my whole face an inch or two under the billowing waves.

"No, no, Betsy," Miss Folgil would scream through her megaphone, as I felt the water rush into my lungs. "No, no, you must keep the head a little higher." At this point I would begin to kick and struggle, and generally the pupil would have to let go while I came up for air. Miss Folgil was always very stern with me.

"Ruth," she would shriek from her boat, "I insist! You must allow Betsy to tow you all the way in. We come to Struggling in Lesson Six."

This was but the mere beginning, however. A few lessons later we came to the section of the course where we learned how to undress under water in forty seconds. Perhaps I should say we came to the point where the *rest* of the pupils learned how to get rid of shoes and such while holding their breaths. I never did.

There was quite a little ceremony connected with this part of the course. Miss Folgil, and some lucky creature named as timekeeper and armed with a stopwatch, rowed the prospective victim out to deep water. The pupil, dressed in high, laced tennis shoes, long stockings, heavy bloomers, and a middy blouse, then stood poised at the end of the boat. When the timekeeper yelled "Go!" the future boon to mankind dived into the water and, while holding her breath under the surface, unlaced her shoes and stripped down to her bathing suit. Miss Folgil never explained what connection, if any, this curious rite had with saving human lives.

I had no middy of my own, so I borrowed one of my sister's. My sister was a slender little thing and I was, as I said, robust, which puts it politely. Eileen had some trouble wedging me into that middy, and once in it I looked like a stuffed sausage. It never occurred to me how hard it was going to be to get that middy off, especially when it was wet and slippery.

As we rowed out for my ordeal by undressing, Miss Folgil was snappish and bored.

"Hurry up," she said, looking irritated. "Let's get this over with quick. I don't think you're ready to pass the test, anyway."

I was good and mad when I jumped off the boat, and determined to Make Good and show that old Miss Folgil, whom I was beginning to dislike thoroughly. As soon as I was under water, I got my shoes off, and I had no trouble with the bloomers or stockings. I was just beginning to run out of breath when I held up my arms and started to pull off the middy.

Now, the middy, in the event you don't understand the principle of this girl-child garment, is made with a small head opening, long sleeves, and no front opening. You pull it on and off over your head. You do if you are lucky, that is. I got the middy just past my neck so that my face was covered with heavy linen cloth, when it stuck.

I pulled frantically and my lungs started to burst. Finally I thought the hell with the test, the hell with saving other people's lives, anyway. I came to the surface, a curious sight, my head enfolded in a water-soaked middy blouse. I made a brief sound, a desperate glub-glub, a call for help. My arms were stuck in the middy and I couldn't swim. I went down. I breathed in large quantities of water and linen cloth.

I came up again, making final frantic appeals. Four feet away sat a professional lifesaver, paying absolutely no attention to somebody drowning right under her nose. I went down again, struggling with last panic-stricken fever-ishness, fighting water and a middy blouse for my life. At this point the timekeeper pointed out to Miss Folgil that I had been under water for eighty-five seconds, which was quite a time for anybody. Miss Folgil was very annoyed, as she hated to get her bathing suit wet, but, a thoughtful teacher, she picked up her megaphone, shouted to the rest of the class on the beach to watch, and dived in after me.

If I say so myself, I gave her quite a time rescuing me. I presented a new and different problem, and probably am written up in textbooks now under the heading "What to Do When the Victim Is Entangled in a Tight Middy Blouse." Miss Folgil finally towed my still-breathing body over to the boat, reached for her bowie knife, which she carried on a ring with her whistle, and cut Eileen's middy straight up the front. Then she towed me with Hold No. 2 right in to the shore and delivered me up to the class for artificial respiration. I will never forgive the Red Cross for that terrible trip through the water, when I might have been hoisted into the boat and rowed in except for Miss Folgil's overdeveloped sense of drama and pedagogy.

I tried to quit the lifesaving class after that, but the head councilor at the camp said I must keep on, to show that I was the kind of girl who always finished what she planned to do. Otherwise, she assured me, I would be a weak character and never amount to anything when I grew up.

So I stayed for Lesson 6: "Struggling." After that I didn't care if I never amounted to anything when I grew up. In fact, I hoped I wouldn't. It would serve everybody right, especially Miss Folgil. I came a little late to the class session that day and missed the discussion of theory, always held on the beach before the actual practice in the lake. That was just my hard luck. I was always a child of misfortune. I wonder that I survived my youth at all.

"We were waiting for you, Ruth," Miss Folgil chirped cheerily to me as I arrived, sullen and downcast, at the little group of earnest students sitting on the sand.

"What for?" I said warily. I was determined not to be a guinea pig any more. The last wave had washed over my helpless face.

"You swim out," Miss Folgil went on, ignoring my bad temper, "until you are in deep water—about twelve feet will do. Then you begin to flail around and shout for help. One of the students will swim out to you."

All of this sounded familiar and terrible. I had been doing that for days, and getting water in my nose for my pains.

"But when the student arrives," Miss Folgil went on, "you must not allow her to simply tow you away. You must struggle, just as hard as you can. You must try to clutch her by the head, you must try to twine your legs about her, and otherwise hamper her in trying to save you."

Now, *this* sounded something like. I was foolishly fired by the attractive thought of getting back at some of the fiends who had been ducking me in the name of science for the past two weeks. Unfortunately, I hadn't studied Chapter 9, entitled "How to Break Holds the Drowning Swimmer Uses." Worse, I hadn't heard Miss Folgil's lecture on "Be Firm with the Panic-Stricken Swimmer—Bet-

ter a Few Bruises Than a Watery Grave." This last was
Miss Folgil's own opinion, of course.

So I swam out to my doom, happy as a lark. Maybelle
Anne Pettijohn, a tall, lean girl who ordinarily wore horn-
rimmed spectacles, was Miss Folgil's choice to rescue Ex-
hibit A, the panic-stricken swimmer.

I laughed when I saw her coming. I thought I could
clean up Maybelle Anne easily enough, but alas, I hadn't
counted on Maybelle Anne's methodical approach to life.
She had read Chapter 9 in our textbook, and she had
listened carefully to Miss Folgil's inspiring words. Besides,
Maybelle Anne was just naturally the kind of girl who ran
around doing people dirty for their own good. "This may
hurt your feelings," she used to say mournfully, "but I feel
I have to tell you . . ."

When Maybelle Anne got near me, I enthusiastically
lunged for her neck and hung on with both hands while
getting her around her waist with my legs. Maybelle Anne
thereupon dug her fingernails into my hands with fero-
cious force, and I let go and swam away, hurt and surprised. This was distinctly not playing fair.

"What's the idea?" I called out.

"It says to do that in the book," Maybelle Anne replied,
treading water.

"Well, you lay off of that stuff," I said, angered, book
or no book. Maybelle Anne was a Girl Scout, too, and I
was shocked to think she'd go around using her fingernails in a fair fight.

"Come on, struggle," Maybelle Anne said, getting
winded from treading water. I swam over, pretty reluctant
and much more wary. Believe it or not, this time Maybelle Anne, who was two medals from being a Beaver or
whatever it is Girl Scouts with a lot of medals get to be,
bit me.

In addition to biting me, Maybelle Anne swung her arm around my neck, with the intention of towing me in to the shore. But I still had plenty of fight left and I had never been so mad in my life. I got Maybelle Anne under water two or three times, and I almost thought I had her when suddenly, to my earnest surprise, she hauled off and hit me as hard as she could, right in the eye. Then she towed me in, triumphant as anything.

Maybelle Anne afterward claimed it was all in the book, and she wouldn't even apologize for my black eye. Eileen and I fixed her, though. We put a little garter snake in her bed and scared the daylights out of her. Maybelle Anne was easy to scare anyway, and really a very disagreeable girl. I used to hope that she would come to a bad end, which, from my point of view, at least, she did. Maybelle Anne grew up to be a Regional Red Cross Lifesaving examiner.

I'll bet she just loves her work.

THE MAN WHO CAME TO DINNER

by George S. Kaufman and Moss Hart

The Man Who Came to Dinner, as nearly everybody knows, is based on the life and times of Alexander Woollcott, who was loved by millions of readers and radio listeners for his sentimental stories about Christmas and small boys and dogs and the like, and who—away from his work—had a tongue as sharp as a sword and bitter as Chinese mustard.

George S. Kaufman and Moss Hart anticipated, of course, that the appearance of the play would send Woollcott into a fury, and cause him to direct some of his special and patented brand of vitriol at them. To their surprise, Woollcott was quite pleased with the play, and even agreed to play the lead. As can be imagined, he was very convincing in the role.

ACT ONE

SCENE I

SCENE: *The curtain rises on the attractive living-room of* MR. *and* MRS. ERNEST W. STANLEY, *in a small town in Ohio. The* STANLEYS *are obviously people of means: the room is large, comfortable, tastefully furnished. Double doors lead into a library* R. *There is a glimpse through an arch* U.R. *of a dining-room at the rear, and we see the steps of a handsome curved staircase,* U.C. *At*

the left side of the room, a bay window. Another arch, U.L. lead-
ing into the hallway. Upstage of the hallway is a swinging door
leading into the pantry. The outer door to the street is off U.L.
The library doors are closed.

MRS. STANLEY *enters from upstairs. As she reaches the lower*
third step the door-bell rings. She pauses a moment, then con-
tinues on her way towards the library. A nurse (MISS PREEN)
in full uniform emerges—scurries rather—out of the room R.,
as the bell rings. An angry voice from within speeds her on her
way: "Great dribbling cow!"

MRS. STANLEY (*eagerly*). How is he? Is he *coming*
out?

(*But* MISS PREEN *has already disappeared into the dining-*
room up R.)

(*Simultaneously the door-bell rings—at the same time a*
young lad of twenty-one, RICHARD STANLEY, *is descending*
the stairs C.)

RICHARD (*crosses to door* L.). I'll go, Mother.

(JOHN, *a white-coated servant, comes hurrying in from*
the library and starts up the stairs, two at a time.)

MRS. STANLEY. What's the matter? What is it, John?

JOHN. They want pillows. (*And he is out of sight.*)

(*Meanwhile* MISS PREEN *is returning to the sick-room.*
She enters as soon as she picks up a tray with a bowl of
cornflakes, off U.R.)

MRS. STANLEY (*to her*). Anything I can do, Miss Preen?

MISS PREEN (*exit to library*). No, thank you.

(*The* VOICE *is heard again as she opens the doors. "Don't*
call yourself a Doctor in my presence! You're a quack if I
ever saw one!")

(RICHARD *returns from the hall* L., *carrying two huge*
packages and a sheaf of cablegrams.)

RICHARD (*crosses to sofa, puts packages on floor* R. *of*
sofa, telegrams on table back of sofa.) Four more cable-

grams and more *packages* . . . Dad is going crazy upstairs,
with that bell ringing all the time.

(*Meanwhile* JUNE, *the daughter of the house, has come
down the stairs* C. *An attractive girl of twenty.*)

(*At the same time the telephone is ringing.* JUNE *crosses*
D.R. *to phone.*)

MRS. STANLEY. Oh, dear! . . . June, will you go? . . .
What did you say, Richard?

RICHARD (*examining the packages*). One's from New
York and one from San Francisco.

MRS. STANLEY. There was something from Alaska early
this morning.

RICHARD. Really?

JUNE (*at the telephone*). Yes? . . . Yes, that's right.

MRS. STANLEY. Who is it?

(*Before* JUNE *can answer, the double doors are opened
again.* MISS PREEN *appears* D.R. *The* VOICE *calls after her:*
"*Doesn't that bird-brain of yours ever function?*")

MISS PREEN (*enters* D.R. *Crosses* L.). I—I'll get them right
away. . . . He wants some Players' Club cigarettes.

MRS. STANLEY. Players' Club?

(JOHN *enters from stairs* C. *with pillows. Gives pillows
to* MISS PREEN D.R., *exits up* R.)

RICHARD. They have 'em at Kitchener's. I'll run down and
get 'em. (*He is off* L.)

JUNE (*still at the phone*). Hello . . . Yes, I'm waiting.

MRS. STANLEY. Tell me, Miss Preen, is he—are they bringing him out soon?

MISS PREEN (*wearily*). We're getting him out of bed
now. He'll be out very soon . . . Oh, thank you. (*This last
is to* JOHN *who has descended the stairs with three or four
pillows.* MISS PREEN *starts off* R.)

MRS. STANLEY. Oh, I'm so glad. He must be very happy.

(*And again we hear the invalid's* VOICE *as* MISS PREEN

passes into the room, R. *"Trapped like a rat in this hell-hole! Take your fish-hooks off me!"*)

JUNE (*at the phone.*) Hello . . . Yes, he's here, but he can't come to the phone right now . . . London? (*She covers the transmitter with her hand.*) It's London calling Mr. Whiteside.

MRS. STANLEY. My, my!

JUNE (*at phone*). Two o'clock? Yes, I think he could talk then. All right. (*She hangs up.*) Well, who do you think that was? Mr. H. G. Wells from London.

MRS. STANLEY (*wild-eyed*). H. G. Wells? On *our* telephone?

(*The door-bell again.*)

JUNE (*crosses* L. *to door* L. *Exit*). I'll go. This is certainly a *busy house.*

(*Meantime* SARAH, *the cook, has come from the dining-room up* R. *with a pitcher of orange juice.*)

SARAH. I got his orange juice.

MRS. STANLEY (*as* SARAH *knocks on double doors* D.R.). Oh, that's fine, Sarah. Is it fresh?

SARAH. Yes, ma'am. (*She knocks on the door.*)

(*The doors are opened;* SARAH *hands the orange juice to the nurse. The* VOICE *roars once more: "You have the touch of a sex-starved cobra!"*)

SARAH (*beaming*). His voice is just the same as on the radio. (*She disappears into the dining-room as* JUNE *returns from the entrance hall,* L., *ushering in two friends of her mother's,* MRS. DEXTER *and* MRS. MCCUTCHEON. *One is carrying a flowering plant, partially wrapped; the other is holding, with some care, what turns out to be a jar of calf's-foot jelly.*)

THE LADIES (*enter* L. *Cross to* C.). Good morning.

MRS. STANLEY (*to them*). Girls, what do you think? He's getting up and coming out this morning!

MRS. MCCUTCHEON. You don't mean it!

MRS. DEXTER. Can we stay and see him?

MRS. STANLEY. Why, of course—he'd love it. (JUNE *enters* L. *Crosses to stairs.*) Girls, do you know what just happened?

JUNE (*departing upstairs*). I'll be upstairs, Mother, if you want me.

MRS. STANLEY. What? . . . Oh, yes. June, tell your father he'd better come down, will you? Mr. Whiteside is coming out.

JUNE. Yes, Mother. (*She exits upstairs.*)

MRS. DEXTER. Is he really coming out this morning? I brought him a plant—do you think it's all right if I give it to him?

MRS. STANLEY. Why, I think that would be lovely.

MRS. MCCUTCHEON. And some calf's-foot jelly.

MRS. STANLEY. Why, how nice! Who do you think was on the phone just now? H. G. Wells, from London. And look at those cablegrams. (*The* LADIES *cross* L.) He's had calls and messages from all over this country and Europe. The *New York Times*—and Felix Frankfurter, and Dr. Dafoe, the Mount Wilson Observatory—I just can't tell you what's been going on, I'm simply exhausted. (*Crosses* R., *sits chair* R.C.)

MRS. DEXTER (*crossing to* MRS. STANLEY R.). There's a big piece about it in this week's *Time*. Did you see it?

MRS. STANLEY. No—really?

MRS. MCCUTCHEON (*crosses* R., *gives* MRS. DEXTER *calf's-foot jelly, reads from* Time.) Your name's in it too, Daisy. Listen: "Portly Sheridan Whiteside, critic, lecturer, wit, radio orator, intimate friend of the great and near great, last week found his celebrated wit no weapon with which to combat an injured hip. The Falstaffian Mr. Whiteside, trekking across the country on one of his annual lecture tours, met his Waterloo in the shape of a small piece of ice on the doorstep of Mr. and Mrs. Ernest W. Stanley, of Mesalia, Ohio. Result: Cancelled lectures and disappointment to thousands of adoring clubwomen in Omaha, Denver, and points West. Further result: The idol of the air waves rests until further notice in home of surprised Mr. and Mrs. Stanley. Possibility: Christmas may be postponed this year." What's *that* mean?

MRS. STANLEY. Why, what do you think of that? (*She takes mazagine: reads.*) "A small piece of ice on the doorstep of Mr. and Mrs. . . ." Think of it!

MRS. McCUTCHEON (*crosses* L. *to sofa* D.L., *sits*). Of course if it were *my* house, Daisy, I'd have a bronze plate put on the step, right where he fell. (MRS. DEXTER *eases back of couch.*)

MRS. STANLEY. Well, of course, I felt terrible about it. He just never goes to dinner anywhere, and he finally agreed to come here, and then *this* had to happen. Poor Mr. Whiteside! But it's going to be so wonderful having him with us, even for a little while. Just think of it! We'll sit around in the evening, and discuss books and plays, all the great people he's known. And he'll talk in that wonderful way of his. He may even read "Good-bye, Mr. Chips" to us.

(MR. STANLEY, *solid, substantial—the American business man—is descending the stairs* C.)

STANLEY (*coming down* C.). Daisy, I can't wait any longer. If Mr. Whiteside—ah, good morning, ladies.

LADIES. Good morning.

MRS. STANLEY (*rises, crosses* C.). Ernest, he's coming out any minute, and H. G. Wells telephoned from London, and we're in *Time*. Look. (*She hands* Time *to* STANLEY.)

STANLEY (*as he hands the magazine back to her*). I don't like this kind of publicity at all, Daisy. When do you suppose he's going to leave?

MRS. STANLEY. Well, he's only getting up this morning—after all, he's had quite a shock, and he's been in bed for two full weeks. He'll certainly have to rest a few days, Ernest.

STANLEY. Well, I'm sure it's a great honor his being in the house, but it *is* a little upsetting—phone going all the time, bells ringing, messenger boys running in and out—(*Out of the sick-room comes a business-like-looking young woman about thirty, with letters and notebook. Her name is* MARGARET CUTLER—MAGGIE *to her friends.*)

MAGGIE (*closing library doors*). Pardon me, Mrs. Stanley—have the cigarettes come yet? (STANLEY *eases* U.L.)

MRS. STANLEY (*crosses* R.). They're on the way, Miss Cutler. My son went for them.

MAGGIE (*crosses* L. *to chair* R.). Thank you.

MRS. STANLEY. Ah—this is Miss Cutler, Mr. Whiteside's secretary.

MAGGIE. How do you do. May I move this chair?

MRS. STANLEY (*all eagerness*). You mean he's coming out now?

(JOHN *appears in doorway up* R.C.)

MAGGIE (*moves chair up* C. *of desk*). (*Quietly.*) He is indeed.

MRS. MCCUTCHEON (*rises, crosses* D.L.). He's coming out!

MRS. DEXTER (*crossing to* MRS. MCCUTCHEON D.L.). I can hardly wait!

MRS. STANLEY. Ernest, call June. June! June! Mr. Whiteside is coming out!

JOHN (*beckoning to* SARAH *off* U.R.). Sarah! Sarah! Mr. Whiteside is coming out!

MRS. STANLEY. I'm so excited I just don't know what to do!

MRS. DEXTER. Me too! I know that I'll simply—

(SARAH *and* JOHN *appear in dining-room entrance,* JUNE *on the stairs.* MRS. STANLEY *and the two other ladies are keenly expectant; even* STANLEY *is on the qui vive. The double doors are opened once more and* DR. BRADLEY *appears, bag in hand,* D.R. *He has taken a good deal of punishment, and speaks with a rather false heartiness.*)

MRS. STANLEY. Good morning, Dr. Bradley.

DR. BRADLEY. Good morning, good morning. Well, here we are, merry and bright. Bring our little patient out, Miss Preen.

(*A moment's pause, and then a wheelchair is rolled through the door by the nurse. It is full of pillows, blankets, and* SHERIDAN WHITESIDE. SHERIDAN WHITESIDE *is indeed portly and Falstaffian. He is wearing an elaborate velvet smoking-jacket and a very loud tie, and he looks like every caricature ever drawn of him. There is a hush as the wheelchair rolls into the room* D.R. *Welcoming smiles break over every face. The chair comes to a halt;* WHITESIDE *looks slowly around, into each and every beaming face. His fingers drum for a moment on the arm of the chair. He looks slowly around once more.* MAGGIE *comes* D.R. DR. BRADLEY *crosses to the wheelchair, then* MRS. STANLEY. *She laughs nervously. And then* HE *speaks.*)

WHITESIDE (R.C., *quietly to* MAGGIE). I may vomit.

MRS. STANLEY (*with a nervous little laugh*). Good morning, Mr. Whiteside. I'm Mrs. Ernest Stanley—remember? And this is Mr. Stanley.

STANLEY (*coming to* D.C.). How do you do, Mr. Whiteside? I hope that you are better.

WHITESIDE. Thank you. I am suing you for a hundred and fifty thousand dollars.

STANLEY. How's that? What?

WHITESIDE. I said I am suing you for a hundred and fifty thousand dollars.

MRS. STANLEY. You mean—because you fell on our steps, Mr. Whiteside?

WHITESIDE. Samuel J. Liebowitz will explain it to you in court. Who are those two harpies standing there like the kiss of death? (MRS. MCCUTCHEON, *with a little gasp, drops the calf's-foot jelly. It smashes to the floor.*)

MRS. MCCUTCHEON. Oh, dear! My calf's-foot jelly.

WHITESIDE. Made from your own foot, I have no doubt. And now, Mrs. Stanley, I have a few small matters to take up with you. Since this corner druggist at my elbow tells me that I shall be confined to this mouldy mortuary for at least another ten days, due entirely to your stupidity and negligence, I shall have to carry on my activities as best I can. I shall require the exclusive use of this room, as well as that drafty sewer which you call the library. I want no one to come in or out while I am in this room.

STANLEY. What do you mean, sir?

MRS. STANLEY (*stunned*). We have to go up the stairs to get to our rooms, Mr. Whiteside.

WHITESIDE. Isn't there a back entrance?

MRS. STANLEY. Why—yes.

WHITESIDE. Then use that. I shall also require a room for my secretary, Miss Cutler. Let me see. I will have a great many incoming and outgoing calls, so please do not use the telephone. I sleep until noon and must have quiet through the house until that hour. There will be five for lunch today. Where is the cook?

STANLEY. Mr. Whiteside, if I may interrupt for a moment—

WHITESIDE. You may not, sir. Will you take your clammy hand off my chair? (*This last to* MISS PREEN *as she arranges his pillow.*) . . . And now will you all leave quietly, or must I ask my secretary to pass among you with a baseball bat?

(MRS. DEXTER *and* MRS. MCCUTCHEON *are beating a hasty retreat,* MRS. DEXTER's *gift still in her hand.*)

MRS. MCCUTCHEON. Well—good-bye, Daisy. We'll call you— Oh, no, we mustn't use the phone. Well—we'll see you.

MRS. DEXTER. Good-bye. (*Both exit up* L.)

STANLEY (*boldly*). Now look here, Mr. Whiteside—

WHITESIDE. There is nothing to discuss, sir. Considering the damage I have suffered at your hands, I am asking very little. Good day.

STANLEY (*controlling himself, crosses* L., *exit* L.) I'll call you from the office later, Daisy.

WHITESIDE. Not on this phone, please.

(STANLEY *gives him a look, but goes.*)

WHITESIDE. Here is the menu for lunch. (*He extends a slip of paper to* MRS. STANLEY.)

MRS. STANLEY. But—I've already ordered lunch.

WHITESIDE. It will be sent up to you on a tray. I am using the dining-room for my guests . . . Where are those cigarettes?

MRS. STANLEY (*eases up*). Why—my son went for them. I don't know why he—here, Sarah. Here is the menu for lunch. (*She hands* SARAH *the luncheon slip, when she has crossed to* MRS. STANLEY.) I'll—have mine upstairs on a tray. (SARAH *and* JOHN *depart up* R.)

WHITESIDE (*to* JUNE, *who has been posed on the landing during all this*). Young lady, I cannot stand indecision. Will you either go up those stairs or come down them?

(JUNE *is about to speak, decides against it and ascends the stairs with a good deal of spirit.*)

(MRS. STANLEY *is hovering uncertainly on the steps as* RICHARD *returns with the cigarettes.*)

RICHARD (*crosses to* R.C.). Oh, good morning, Mr. White-

side. Here are the cigarettes.—I'm sorry I was so long
—I had to go to three different stores.

WHITESIDE. How did you travel? By oxcart? You were
gone long enough to have a baby. (RICHARD *is considerably
taken aback. His eyes go to his mother, who motions to him
to come up the stairs. They disappear together, their eyes
unsteadily on* WHITESIDE.) Is there a man in the world who
suffers as I do from the gross inadequacies of the human
race! (*To* MISS PREEN *who is fussing around the chair
again tucking blanket about him.*) Take those canal boats
away from me! (*She obeys hastily.*) Go in and read the life
of Florence Nightingale and learn how unfitted you are for
your chosen profession.

(MISS PREEN *glares at him, but goes* D.R., *leaves doors
open.*)

BRADLEY (*heartily—coming down to* L. *of chair*). Well,
I think I can safely leave you in Miss Cutler's capable
hands. Shall I look in again this afternoon?

WHITESIDE. If you do, I shall spit right in your eye.

BRADLEY. Ah! What a sense of humor you writers have!
By the way, it isn't really worth mentioning, but—I've been
doing a little writing myself. About my medical experiences.

WHITESIDE (*quietly*). Am I to be spared nothing?

BRADLEY. Would it be too much to ask you to—glance
over it while you're here?

WHITESIDE (*eyes half closed, as though the pain were too
exquisite to bear*). Trapped.

BRADLEY (*delving into his bag*). Well! I just happen to
have a copy with me. (*He brings out a tremendous manuscript, places it on* WHITESIDE's *lap.*) "The Story of an Humble Practitioner, or Forty Years an Ohio Doctor."

WHITESIDE. I shall drop everything.

BRADLEY (*crossing* L.). Thank you, and I hope you like it.

Well, see you on the morrow. Keep that hip quiet and don't forget those little pills. Good-bye. (*He goes up* L.)

WHITESIDE (*annoyed at* BRADLEY). Oh-h! (*Handing the manuscript to* MAGGIE *who places it on chest* D.R.) Maggie, will you take "Forty Years Below the Navel" or whatever it's called?

MAGGIE (*crossing* L. *to* C., *surveying him*). Well, I must say you have certainly behaved with all your accustomed grace and charm.

WHITESIDE. Look here, Puss—I am in no mood to discuss my behavior, good or bad.

MAGGIE. These people have done everything in their power to make you comfortable. And they happen, God knows why, to look upon you with certain wonder and admiration.

WHITESIDE. If they had looked a little more carefully at their doorstep I would not be troubling them now. I did not wish to cross their cheerless threshold. I was hounded and badgered into it. I now find myself, after two weeks of racking pain, accused of behaving without charm. What would you have me do? Kiss them?

MAGGIE (*giving up, crossing to* WHITESIDE). Very well, Sherry. After ten years I should have known better than to try to do anything about your manners. But when I finally give up this job I may write a book about it all. "Cavalcade of Insult" or "Through the Years With Prince Charming." (*Tosses him letters.*)

WHITESIDE. Listen, Repulsive, you are tied to me with an umbilical cord made of piano-wire. And now if we may dismiss the subject of my charm, for which, incidentally, I receive fifteen hundred dollars per appearance, (*Enter* HARRIET L.) possibly we can go to work . . . Oh, no, we can't. Yes? (MAGGIE *crosses* R. *to* D.R.)

(*This last is addressed to a wraith-like lady of uncertain years, who has more or less floated into the room. She is carrying a large spray of holly, and her whole manner suggests something not quite of this world.*)

HARRIET (*crosses to him. Her voice seems to float, too*). My name is Harriet Stanley. I know you are Sheridan Whiteside. I saw this holly, framed green against the pine trees. I remembered what you had written about "Tess" and "Jude the Obscure." It was the nicest present I could bring you. (*She places the holly in his lap, and exits upstairs* c.)

WHITESIDE (*his eyes following her*). For God's sake, what was that?

MAGGIE (*crosses* L. *to packages by sofa, takes them to chair up* R.) That was Mr. Stanley's sister, Harriet. I've talked to her a few times—she's quite strange.

WHITESIDE. Strange? She's right out of "The Hound of the Baskervilles" . . . You know, I've seen that face before somewhere.

MAGGIE (*as she puts packages on chair* U.C.). Nonsense. You couldn't have.

WHITESIDE (*dismissing it*). Oh, well! Let's get down to work. (*He hands her the armful of holly.*) Here! Press this in the Doctor's book. (MAGGIE *places holly on sofa. He picks up the first of a pile of letters.*) I see no reason why I should endorse Maiden Form Brassieres. (*He crumples up letter and drops it.*) If young men keep asking me how to become dramatic critics— (*He tears up letter and drops it on the floor.*)

MAGGIE (*who has picked up the little sheaf of messages from the table back of sofa*). Here are some telegrams.

WHITESIDE (*a letter in his hand*). What date is this?

MAGGIE. December tenth. (MAGGIE *sits sofa.*)

WHITESIDE. Send a wire to Columbia Broadcasting: "You can schedule my Christmas Eve broadcast from the New

York studio, as I shall return East instead of proceeding to Hollywood. Stop. For special New Year's Eve broadcast will have as my guests Jascha Heifetz, Katharine Cornell, Schiaparelli, the Lunts, and Dr. Alexis Carrel, with Anthony Eden on short wave from England. Whiteside."

MAGGIE. Are you sure you'll be all right by Christmas, Sherry?

WHITESIDE. Of course I will. Send a cable to Sacha Guitry: "Will be in Paris June ninth. Dinner seven-thirty. Whiteside." . . . Wire to *Harper's Magazine:* "Do not worry, Stinky. Copy will arrive. Whiteside." . . . Send a cable to the Maharajah of Jehraput, Bombay: "Dear Boo-Boo: Schedule changed. Can you meet me Calcutta July twelfth? Dinner eight-thirty. Whiteside." . . . Arturo Toscanini. Where *is* he?

MAGGIE. I'll find him.

WHITESIDE. "Counting on you January 4th Metropolitan Opera House my annual benefit Home for Paroled Convicts. As you know this is a very worthy cause and close to my heart. Tibbett, Rethberg, Martinelli, and Flagstad have promised me personally to appear. Will you have quiet supper with me and Ethel Barrymore afterwards? Whiteside." (*Telephone rings.*) (MAGGIE *crosses back of* WHITESIDE *to phone* D.R.) If that's for Mrs. Stanley, tell them she's too drunk to talk.

MAGGIE (*at phone* D.R.). Hello . . . what? . . . Hollywood?

WHITESIDE. If it's Goldwyn, hang up.

MAGGIE. Hello, Banjo! (*Her face lights up.*)

WHITESIDE. Banjo! Give me that phone!

MAGGIE. Banjo, you old so-and-so! How are you, darling?

WHITESIDE. Come on—give me that!

MAGGIE. Shut up, Sherry! . . . Are you coming East, Banjo? I miss you . . . Oh, he's going to live.

WHITESIDE. Stop driveling and give me the phone.

MAGGIE (*hands him phone—stands back of wheelchair*). In fact, he's screaming at me now. Here he is.

WHITESIDE (*taking the phone*). How are you, you fawn's behind? And what are you giving me for Christmas? (*He roars with laughter at* BANJO's *answer.*) What news, Banjo, my boy? How's the picture coming? . . . How are Wacko and Sloppo? . . . No, no, I'm all right . . . Yes, I'm in very good hands. I've got the best horse doctor in town . . . What about you? Having any fun? . . . Playing any cribbage? . . . What? (*Again he laughs loudly.*) . . . Well, don't take all his money—leave a little bit for me. . . . You're what? . . . Having your portrait painted? By whom? Milt Gross? . . . Not really? . . . No, I'm going back to New York from here. I'll be there for twelve days, and then I go to Dartmouth for the Drama Festival. You wouldn't understand . . . Well, I can't waste my time talking to Hollywood riff-raff. Kiss Louella Parsons for me. Good-bye. (*He hangs up and turns to* MAGGIE. MAGGIE *puts phone on table* D.R.) He took fourteen hundred dollars from Sam Goldwyn at cribbage last night, and Sam said "Banjo, I will never play garbage with you again."

MAGGIE (*crossing* L. *to* L.C.). What's all this about his having his portrait painted?

WHITESIDE. M-m, Salvador Dali. (MISS PREEN *enters* D.R.) That's all that face of his needs—a Surrealist to paint it. . . . What do *you* want now, Miss Bed Pan?

(MAGGIE *crosses to table back of couch* L.)

(*This is addressed to* MISS PREEN *who has returned somewhat apprehensively to the room.*)

MISS PREEN. It's—it's your pills. One every forty-five minutes. (*She drops them into his lap and hurries out of the room—Exit* D.R.)

(MAGGIE, *back of couch* L., *opens cable.*)

WHITESIDE (*looking after her*). . . . Now where were we?

MAGGIE (*the messages in her hand, crosses to* C.). Here's a cable from that dear friend of yours, Lorraine Sheldon.

WHITESIDE. Let me see it.

MAGGIE (*reading message, in a tone that gives* MISS SHELDON *none the better of it. Crosses to* C.). "Sherry, my poor sweet lamb, have been in Scotland on a shooting party with Lord and Lady Cunard and only just heard of your poor sweet hip." (MAGGIE *gives a faint raspberry, then reads on.*) "Am down here in Surrey with Lord Bottomley. Sailing Wednesday on the *Normandie* and cannot wait to see my poor sweet Sherry. Your blossom girl, Lorraine." . . . In the words of the master, I may vomit.

WHITESIDE. Don't be bitter, Puss, just because Lorraine is more beautiful than you are.

MAGGIE. Lorraine Sheldon is a very fair example of that small but vicious circle you move in.

WHITESIDE. Pure sex jealousy if I ever saw it . . . Give me the rest of those.

MAGGIE (*mumbling to herself, crossing* R. *and handing him cables*). Lorraine Sheldon . . . Lord Bottomley . . . My Aunt Fanny. (*Crossing* U.C.)

WHITESIDE (*who has opened the next message*). Ah! It's from Destiny's Tot.

MAGGIE (*crossing to* WHITESIDE). (*Peering over his shoulder.*) Oh, England's little Rover Boy?

WHITESIDE. Um-hm. (*He reads.*) "Treacle face, what is this I hear about a hip fractured in some bordello brawl? Does this mean our Hollywood Christmas Party is off? Finished the new play in Pago-Pago and it's superb. Myself and a ukulele leave Honolulu tomorrow in that order. By the way, the Sultan of Zanzibar wants to meet Ginger Rogers. Let's face it. Oscar Wilde."

MAGGIE (*crossing* L. *to couch, sits*). He does travel, doesn't he. You know, it would be nice if the world went around Beverly Carlton for a change.

WHITESIDE. Hollywood next week—why couldn't he stop over on his way to New York? Send him a cable. "Beverly Carlton, Royal Hawaiian Hotel, Honolulu." (*The door-bell rings.* WHITESIDE *is properly annoyed.*) If these people intend to have their friends using the front door . . . (JOHN *enters up* L.)

MAGGIE. What do you want them to do—use a rope ladder? (JOHN *at* L.C., *crosses to exit* L.)

WHITESIDE. I will not have a lot of mildewed pus-bags rushing in and out of this house while I am— (*He stops as the voice of* JOHN *is heard at the front door.* "Oh, good morning, Mr. Jefferson." *The answering voice of* MR. JEFFERSON: "*Good morning, John.*") (*Roaring*—MAGGIE *rises, crosses to up* L.) There's nobody home! The Stanleys have been arrested for whiteslavery! Go away! (*But the visitor, meanwhile, has already appeared in the archway.* JEFFERSON *is an interesting-looking young man in his early thirties.*)

JEFFERSON (*crossing to her, back of couch*). Good morning, Mr. Whiteside. I'm Jefferson, of the Mesalia *Journal.*

WHITESIDE (*sotto voce, to* MAGGIE). Get rid of him.

MAGGIE (*brusquely*). I'm sorry—Mr. Whiteside is seeing no one.

JEFFERSON. Really?

MAGGIE. So will you please excuse us? Good day.

JEFFERSON (*not giving up*). Mr. Whiteside seems to be sitting up and taking notice.

MAGGIE. I'm afraid he's not taking notice of the Mesalia *Journal.* Do you mind?

JEFFERSON (*sizing up* MAGGIE). You know, if I'm going to be insulted I'd like it to be by Mr. Whiteside himself. I never did like carbon copies.

WHITESIDE (*looking around; interested*). M-m, touché, if I ever heard one. And in Mesalia too, Maggie, dear.

MAGGIE (*still on the job*). Will you please leave?

JEFFERSON (*ignoring her. Crosses to* C. MAGGIE *crosses to* R.C.). How about an interview, Mr. Whiteside?

WHITESIDE. I never give them. Go away.

JEFFERSON. Mr. Whiteside, if I don't get this interview, I lose my job.

WHITESIDE. That would be quite all right with me.

JEFFERSON. Now you don't mean that, Mr. Whiteside. You used to be a newspaper man yourself. You know what editors are like. Well, mine's the toughest one that ever lived.

WHITESIDE. You won't get around me that way. If you don't like him, get off the paper.

JEFFERSON. Yes, but I happen to think it's a good paper. William Allen White could have got out of Emporia, but he didn't.

WHITESIDE. You have the effrontery, in my presence, to compare yourself with William Allen White?

JEFFERSON. Only in the sense that White stayed in Emporia, and I want to stay here and say what I want to say.

WHITESIDE. Such as what?

JEFFERSON (*crossing to below couch* L.). Well, I can't put it into words, Mr. Whiteside—it'd sound like an awful lot of hooey. But the *Journal* was my father's paper. It's kind of a sentimental point with me, the paper. I'd like to carry on where he left off.

WHITESIDE. Ah—ahh. So you own the paper, eh?

JEFFERSON. That's right.

WHITESIDE. Then this terrifying editor, this dread journalistic Apocalypse is—you yourself?

JEFFERSON. In a word, yes.

WHITESIDE (*chuckles with appreciation*). I see.

MAGGIE (*annoyed, starts off* R.). In the future, Sherry, let me know when you don't want to talk to people, I'll usher them right in. (*She goes into the library* D.R.)

WHITESIDE. Young man, that kind of journalistic trick went out with Richard Harding Davis . . . Come over here. I suppose you've written that novel?

JEFFERSON (*eases* R.). No. I've written that play.

WHITESIDE. Well, I don't want to read it. But you can send me your paper—I'll take a year's subscription. Do you write the editorials, too?

JEFFERSON. Every one of them.

WHITESIDE. I know just what they're like. Ah, me! I'm afraid you're that noble young newspaper man—crusading, idealistic, dull. (*He looks up and down.*) Very good casting, too.

JEFFERSON. You're not bad casting yourself, Mr. Whiteside.

WHITESIDE. We won't discuss it. . . . Ah, do these old eyes see a box of goodies over there? Hand them to me on your way out.

JEFERSON (*crossing* D.R. *to small desk table*). The trouble is, Mr. Whiteside, that your being in this town comes under the heading of news. Practically the biggest news since the depression. So I just got to get a story. (*Crossing to* L. *of* WHITESIDE.) (*As he passes candy.*)

WHITESIDE (*examining the candy*). M-m, pecan butternut fudge.

(MISS PREEN, *on her way to the kitchen with empty plate on tray, from the library* R. *stops short as she sees* WHITESIDE *with a piece of candy in his hand. She leaves doors open.*)

MISS PREEN (*crossing* D.R.). Oh, my! You mustn't eat candy, Mr. Whiteside. It's very bad for you.

WHITESIDE (*turning*). My Great-aunt Jennifer ate a whole box of candy every day of her life. She lived to be a hundred and two, and when she had been dead three days she looked better than you do now.

TROUBLE DOWN AT TUDSLEIGH

by P. G. Wodehouse

P. G. Wodehouse, coeditor of this book and author of its con-
cluding selection, is the acknowledged dean of modern humor
writers, probably the most successful and famous humorist in
the world today. He is the creator of Jeeves, Psmith, Mr. Mul-
liner, Lord Emsworth, Ukridge, and many other famous characters.

Several years ago, Mr. Wodehouse was given an honorary
Doctorate in Literature by Oxford University, the second humorist to be so honored. The first was Mark Twain. This year,
Mr. Wodehouse completes fifty years of writing, his first book
having been published in 1902, when he was twenty-one.

Two EGGS and a couple of Beans were having a leisurely
spot in the smoking room of the Drones Club, when a
Crumpet came in and asked if anybody present wished to
buy a practically new copy of Tennyson's poems. His manner, as he spoke, suggested that he had little hope that
business would result. Nor did it. The two Beans and one
of the Eggs said No. The other Egg merely gave a short,
sardonic laugh.

The Crumpet hastened to put himself right with the
company.

"It isn't mine. It belongs to Freddie Widgeon."

The senior of the two Beans drew his breath in sharply, genuinely shocked.

"You aren't telling us that Freddie Widgeon bought a Tennyson?"

The junior Bean said that this confirmed a suspicion which had long been stealing over him. Poor old Freddie was breaking up.

"Not at all," said the Crumpet. "He had the most excellent motives. The whole thing was a strategic move, and in my opinion a jolly fine strategic move. He did it to boost his stock with the girl."

"What girl?"

"April Carroway. She lived at a place called Tudsleigh down in Worcestershire. Freddie went there for the fishing, and the day he left London he happened to run into his uncle, Lord Blicester, and the latter, learning that he was to be in those parts, told him on no account to omit to look in at Tudsleigh Court and slap his old friend, Lady Carroway, on the back. So Freddie called there on the afternoon of his arrival, to get the thing over; and as he was passing through the garden on his way out he suddenly heard a girl's voice proceeding from the interior of the summerhouse. And so musical was it that he edged a bit closer and shot a glance through the window. And, as he did so, he reeled and came within a toucher of falling."

From where he stood (said the Crumpet) he could see the girl plainly, and she was, he tells me, the absolute ultimate word, the last bubbling cry. She could not have looked better to him if he had drawn up the specifications personally. He was stunned. He had had no idea that there was anything like this on the premises. There and then he abandoned his scheme of spending the next two weeks fishing; for day by day in every way, he realised, he must haunt Tudsleigh Court from now on like a resident spectre.

He had now recovered sufficiently for his senses to function once more, and he gathered that what the girl was doing was reading some species of poetry aloud to a small, grave female kid with green eyes and a turned-up nose who sat at her side. And the idea came to him that it would be a pretty sound scheme if he could find out what this bilge was. For, of course, when it comes to wooing, it's simply half the battle to get a line on the adored object's favourite literature. Ascertain what it is and mug it up and decant an excerpt or two in her presence, and before you can say "What ho!" she is looking on you as a kindred soul and is all over you.

And it was at this point that he had a nice little slice of luck. The girl suddenly stopped reading; and, placing the volume face down on her lap, sat gazing dreamily nor'-nor'-east for a space, as I believe girls frequently do when they strike a particularly juicy bit halfway through a poem. And the next moment Freddie was hareing off to the local post office to wire to London for a *Collected Works of Alfred, Lord Tennyson*. He was rather relieved, he tells me, because, girls being what they are, it might quite easily have been Shelley or even Browning.

Well, Freddie lost no time in putting into operation his scheme of becoming the leading pest of Tudsleigh Court. On the following afternoon he called there again, met Lady Carroway once more, and was introduced to this girl, April, and to the green-eyed kid, who, he learned, was her young sister Prudence. So far, so good. But just as he was starting to direct at April a respectfully volcanic look which would give her some rough kind of preliminary intimation that here came old Colonel Romeo in person, his hostess went on to say something which sounded like "Captain Bradbury," and he perceived with a nasty shock that he was not the only visitor. Seated in a chair with a cup of tea in one hand and half a muffin in the other was an extraordinarily large and beefy bird in tweeds.

"Captain Bradbury, Mr. Widgeon," said Lady Carroway. "Captain Bradbury is in the Indian Army. He is home on leave and has taken a house up the river."

"Oh?" said Freddie, rather intimating by his manner that this was just the dirty sort of trick he would have imagined the other would have played.

"Mr. Widgeon is the nephew of my old friend, Lord Blicester."

"Ah?" said Captain Bradbury, hiding with a hamlike hand a yawn that seemed to signify that Freddie's foul antecedents were of little interest to him. It was plain that this was not going to be one of those sudden friendships. Captain Bradbury was obviously feeling that a world fit for heroes to live in should contain the irreducible minimum of Widgeons; while, as for Freddie, the last person he wanted hanging about the place at this highly critical point in his affairs was a richly tanned military man with deep-set eyes and a natty moustache.

However, he quickly rallied from his momentary agitation. Once that volume of Tennyson came, he felt, he would pretty soon put this bird where he belonged. A natty moustache is not everything. Nor is rich tan. And the same may be said of deep-set eyes. What bungs a fellow over with a refined and poetical girl is Soul. And in the course of the next few days Freddie expected to have soul enough for six. He exerted himself, accordingly, to be the life of the party, and so successful were his efforts that, as they were leaving, Captain Bradbury drew him aside and gave him the sort of look he would have given a Pathan discovered pinching the old regiment's rifles out on the North-Western Frontier. And it was only now that Freddie really began to appreciate the other's physique. He had had no notion that they were making the soldiery so large nowadays.

"Tell me, Pridgeon—"

"Widgeon," said Freddie, to keep the records straight.

"Tell me, Widgeon, are you making a long stay in these parts?"

"Oh yes. Fairly longish."

"I shouldn't."

"You wouldn't?"

"Not if I were you."

"But I like scenery."

"If you got both eyes bunged up, you wouldn't be able to see the scenery."

"Why should I get both eyes bunged up?"

"You might."

"But why?"

"I don't know. You just might. These things happen. Well, good evening, Widgeon," said Captain Bradbury and hopped into his two-seater like a performing elephant alighting on an upturned barrel. And Freddie made his way to the Blue Lion in Tudsleigh village, where he had established his headquarters.

It would be idle to deny that this little chat gave Frederick Widgeon food for thought. He brooded on it over his steak and French-fried that night, and was still brooding on it long after he had slid between the sheets and should have been in a restful sleep. And when morning brought its eggs and bacon and coffee he began to brood on it again.

He's a pretty astute sort of chap, Freddie, and he had not failed to sense the threatening note in the Captain's remarks. And he was somewhat dubious as to what to do for the best. You see, it was the first time anything of this sort had happened to him. I suppose, all in all, Freddie Widgeon has been in love at first sight with possibly twenty-seven girls in the course of his career; but hitherto everything had been what you might call plain sailing. I mean, he would flutter round for a few days and then the girl, incensed by some floater on his part or possibly merely unable to stand the sight of him any longer, would throw him out on his left ear, and that would be that. Everything pleasant and agreeable and orderly, as you might say. But this was different. Here he had come up against a new element, the jealous rival, and it was beginning to look not so good.

It was the sight of Tennyson's poems that turned the scale. The volume had arrived early on the previous day, and already he had mugged up two thirds of the "Lady of Shalott." And the thought that, if he were to oil out now, all this frightful sweat would be so much dead loss, decided the issue. That afternoon he called once more at Tudsleigh Court, prepared to proceed with the matter along the lines originally laid out. And picture his astonishment and delight when he discovered that Captain Bradbury was not among those present.

There are very few advantages about having a military man as a rival in your wooing, but one of these is that every now and then such a military man has to pop up to London to see the blokes at the War Office. This Captain Bradbury had done today, and it was amazing what a difference his absence made. A gay confidence seemed to fill Freddie as he sat there wolfing buttered toast. He had finished the "Lady of Shalott" that morning and was stuffed to the tonsils with good material. It was only a question of time, he felt, before some chance remark would uncork him and give him the cue to do his stuff.

And presently it came. Lady Carroway, withdrawing

to write letters, paused at the door to ask April if she had any message for her uncle Lancelot.

"Give him my love," said April, "and say I hope he likes Bournemouth."

The door closed. Freddie coughed.

"He's moved, then?" he said.

"I beg your pardon?"

"Just a spot of persiflage. Lancelot, you know. Tennyson, you know. You remember in the 'Lady of Shalott' Lancelot was putting in most of his time at Camelot."

The girl stared at him, dropping a slice of bread-and-butter in her emotion.

"You don't meant to say you read Tennyson, Mr. Widgeon?"

"Me?" said Freddie. "Tennyson? Read Tennyson? Me read Tennyson? Well, well, well! Bless my soul! Why, I know him by heart—some of him."

"So do I! 'Break, break, break, on your cold grey stones, oh Sea . . .'"

"Quite. Or take the 'Lady of Shalott.'"

"'I hold it truth with him who sings . . .'"

"So do I, absolutely. And then, again, there's the 'Lady of Shalott.' Dashed extraordinary that you should like Tennyson, too."

"I think he's wonderful."

"What a lad! That 'Lady of Shalott!' Some spin on the ball there."

"It's so absurd, the way people sneer at him nowadays."

"The silly bounders. Don't know what's good for them."

"He's my favourite poet."

"Mine, too. Any bird who could write the 'Lady of Shalott' gets the cigar or coconut, according to choice, as far as I'm concerned."

They gazed at one another emotionally.

"Well, I'd never have thought it," said April.

"Why not?"

"I mean, you gave me the impression of being—well, rather the dancing, night-club sort of man."

"What! Me? Night clubs? Good gosh! Why, my idea of a happy evening is to curl up with Tennyson's latest."

"Don't you love 'Locksley Hall'?"

"Oh, rather. And the 'Lady of Shalott.' "

"And 'Maud'?"

"Aces," said Freddie. "And the 'Lady of Shalott.' "

"How fond you seem of the 'Lady of Shalott'!"

"Oh, I am."

"So am I, of course. The river here always reminds me so much of that poem."

"Why, of course it does!" said Freddie. "I've been trying to think all the time why it seemed so dashed familiar. And, talking of the river, I suppose you wouldn't care for a row up it tomorrow?"

The girl looked doubtful.

"Tomorrow?"

"My idea was to hire a boat, sling in a bit of chicken and ham and a Tennyson—"

"But I had promised to go to Birmingham tomorrow with Captain Bradbury to help him choose a fishing rod. Still, I suppose, really, any other day would do for that, wouldn't it?"

"Exactly."

"We could go later on."

"Positively," said Freddie. "A good deal later on. Much later on. In fact, the best plan would be to leave it quite open. One o'clock tomorrow, then, at the Town Bridge? Right. Fine. Splendid. Topping. I'll be there with my hair in a braid."

All through the rest of the day Freddie was right in the

pink. Walked on air, you might say. But towards nightfall, as he sat in the bar of the Blue Lion, sucking down a whisky-and-splash and working his way through "Locksley Hall," a shadow fell athwart the table and, looking up, he perceived Captain Bradbury.

"Good evening, Widgeon," said Captain Bradbury.

There is only one word, Freddie tells me, to describe the gallant C.'s aspect at this juncture. It was sinister. His eyebrows had met across the top of his nose, his chin was sticking out from ten to fourteen inches, and he stood there flexing the muscles of his arms, making the while a low sound like the rumbling of an only partially extinct volcano. The impression Freddie received was that at any moment molten lava might issue from the man's mouth, and he wasn't absolutely sure that he liked the look of things.

However, he tried to be as bright as possible.

"Ah, Bradbury!" he replied, with a lilting laugh.

Captain Bradbury's right eyebrow had now become so closely entangled with his left that there seemed to be no hope of ever extricating it without the aid of powerful machinery.

"I understand that you called at Tudsleigh Court today."

"Oh, rather. We missed you, of course, but, nevertheless, a pleasant time was had by all."

"So I gathered. Miss Carroway tells me that you have invited her to picnic up the river with you tomorrow."

"That's right. Up the river. The exact spot."

"You will, of course, send her a note informing her that you are unable to go, as you have been unexpectedly called back to London."

"But nobody's called me back to London."

"Yes, they have. I have."

Freddie tried to draw himself up. A dashed difficult

thing to do, of course, when you're sitting down, and he didn't make much of a job of it.

"I fail to understand you, Bradbury."

"Let me make it clearer," said the Captain. "There is an excellent train in the morning at twelve-fifteen. You will catch it tomorrow."

"Oh yes?"

"I shall call here at one o'clock. If I find that you have not gone, I shall . . . Did I ever happen to mention that I won the Heavyweight Boxing Championship of India last year?"

Freddie swallowed a little thoughtfully.

"You did?"

"Yes."

Freddie pulled himself together.

"The Amateur Championship?"

"Of course."

"I used to go in quite a lot for amateur boxing," said Freddie with a little yawn. "But I got bored with it. Not enough competition. Too little excitement. So I took on pros. But I found them so extraordinarily brittle that I chucked the whole thing. That was when Bulldog Whacker had to go to hospital for two months after one of our bouts. I collect old china now."

Brave words, of course, but he watched his visitor depart with emotions that were not too fearfully bright. In fact, he tells me, he actually toyed for a moment with the thought that there might be a lot to be said for that twelve-fifteen train.

It was but a passing weakness. The thought of April Carroway soon strengthened him once more. He had invited her to this picnic, and he intended to keep the tryst even if it meant having to run like a rabbit every time Captain Bradbury hove in sight. After all, he reflected, it was most improbable that a big heavy fellow like that would be able to catch him.

His frame of mind, in short, was precisely that of the old Crusading Widgeons when they heard that the paynim had been sighted in the offing.

The next day, accordingly, found Freddie seated in a hired rowboat at the landing stage by the Town Bridge. It was a lovely summer morning with all the fixings, such as blue skies, silver wavelets, birds, bees, gentle breezes and what not. He had stowed the luncheon basket in the stern, and was whiling away the time of waiting by brushing up his "Lady of Shalott," when a voice spoke from the steps. He looked up and perceived the kid Prudence gazing down at him with her grave, green eyes.

"Oh, hullo," he said.

"Hullo," said the child.

Since his entry to Tudsleigh Court, Prudence Carroway had meant little or nothing in Freddie's life. He had seen her around, of course, and had beamed at her in a benevolent sort of way, it being his invariable policy to beam benevolently at all relatives and connections of the adored object, but he had scarcely given her a thought. As always on these occasions, his whole attention had been earmarked for the adored one. So now his attitude was rather that of a bloke who wonders to what he is indebted for the honour of this visit.

"Nice day," he said, tentatively.

"Yes," said the kid. "I came to tell you that April can't come."

The sun, which had been shining with exceptional brilliance, seemed to Freddie to slip out of sight like a diving duck.

"You don't mean that!"

"Yes, I do."

"Can't come?"

"No. She told me to tell you she's awfully sorry, but some friends of Mother's have phoned that they are passing through and would like lunch, so she's got to stay on and help cope with them."

"Oh, gosh!"

"So she wants you to take me instead, and she's going to try to come on afterwards. I told her we would lunch near Griggs' Ferry."

Something of the inky blackness seemed to Freddie to pass from the sky. It was a jar, of course, but still, if the girl was going to join him later. . . . And, as for having this kid along, well, even that had its bright side. He could see that it would be by no means a bad move to play the hearty host to this young blighter. Reports of the lavishness of his hospitality and the suavity of his demeanour would get round to April and might do him quite a bit of good. It is a recognized fact that a lover is never wasting his time when he lushes up the little sister.

"All right," he said. "Hop in."

So the kid hopped, and they shoved off. There wasn't anything much in the nature of intellectual conversation for the first ten minutes or so, because there was a fairish amount of traffic on the river at this point and the kid, who had established herself at the steering apparatus, seemed to have a rather sketchy notion of the procedure. As she explained to Freddie after they had gone about halfway through a passing barge, she always forgot which of the ropes it was that you pulled when you wanted to go to the right. However, the luck of the Widgeons saw them through and eventually they came, still afloat, to the unfrequented upper portions of the stream. Here in some mysterious way the rudder fell off, and after that it was all much easier. And it was at this point that the kid, having no longer anything to occupy herself with, reached out and picked up the book.

"Hullo! Are you reading Tennyson?"

"I was before we started, and I shall doubtless dip into him again later on. You will generally find me having a pop at the bard under advisement when I get a spare five minutes."

"You don't mean to say you like him?"

"Of course I do. Who doesn't?"

"I don't. April's been making me read him, and I think he's soppy."

"He is not soppy at all. Dashed beautiful."

"But don't you think his girls are awful blisters?"

Apart from his old crony, the Lady of Shalott, Freddie had not yet made the acquaintance of any of the women in Tennyson's poems, but he felt very strongly that if they were good enough for April Carroway, they were good enough for a green-eyed child with freckles all over her nose, and he said as much, rather severely.

"Tennyson's heroines," said Freddie, "are jolly fine specimens of pure, sweet womanhood, so get that into your nut, you soulless kid. If you behaved like a Tennyson heroine you would be doing well."

"Which of them?"

"Any of them. Pick 'em where you like. You can't go wrong. How much further to this Ferry place?"

"It's round the next bend."

It was naturally with something of a pang that Freddie tied the boat up at their destination. Not only was this Griggs' Ferry a lovely spot, it was in addition completely deserted. There was a small house through the trees, but it showed no signs of occupancy. The only living thing for miles around appeared to be an elderly horse which was taking a snack on the river bank. In other words, if only

April had been there and the kid hadn't, they would have been alone together with no human eye to intrude upon their sacred solitude. They could have read Tennyson to each other till they were blue in the face, and not a squawk from a soul.

A saddening thought, of course. Still, as the row had given him a nice appetite, he soon dismissed these wistful yearnings and started unpacking the luncheon basket. And at the end of about twenty minutes, during which period nothing had broken the stillness but the sound of champing jaws, he felt that it would not be amiss to chat with his little guest.

"Had enough?" he asked.

"No," said the kid. "But there isn't any more."

"You seem to tuck away your food all right."

"The girls at school used to call me Teresa the Tapeworm," said the kid with a touch of pride.

It suddenly struck Freddie as a little odd that with July only half over this child should be at large. The summer holidays, as he remembered it, always used to start about the first of August.

"Why aren't you at school now?"

"I was bunked last month."

"Really?" said Freddie, interested. "They gave you the push, did they? What for?"

"Shooting pigs."

"Shooting pigs?"

"With a bow and arrow. One pig, that is to say. Percival. He belonged to Miss Maitland, the head-mistress. Do you ever pretend to be people in books?"

"Never. And don't stray from the point at issue. I want to get to the bottom of this thing about the pig."

"I'm not straying from the point at issue. I was playing William Tell."

"The old apple-knocker, you mean?"

"The man who shot an apple off his son's head. I tried to get one of the girls to put the apple on her head, but she wouldn't, so I went down to the pigsty and put it on Percival's. And the silly goop shook it off and started to eat it just as I was shooting, which spoiled my aim and I got him on the left ear. He was rather vexed about it. So was Miss Maitland. Especially as I was supposed to be disgraced at the time, because I had set the dormitory on fire the night before."

Freddie blinked a bit.

"You set the dormitory on fire?"

"Yes."

"Any special reason, or just a passing whim?"

"I was playing Florence Nightingale."

"Florence Nightingale?"

"The Lady with the Lamp. I dropped the lamp."

"Tell me," said Freddie. "This Miss Maitland of yours. What colour is her hair?"

"Grey."

"I thought as much. And now, if you don't mind, switch off the childish prattle for the nonce. I feel a restful sleep creeping over me."

"My uncle Joe says that people who sleep after lunch have got fatty degeneration of the heart."

"Your uncle Joe is an ass," said Freddie.

How long it was before Freddie awoke, he could not have said. But when he did the first thing that impressed itself upon him was that the kid was no longer in sight, and this worried him a bit. I mean to say, a child who, on her own showing, plugged pigs with arrows and set fires to dormitories was not a child he was frightfully keen on having roam about the countryside at a time when he was supposed to be more or less in charge of her. He got

up, feeling somewhat perturbed, and started walking about
and bellowing her name.

Rather a chump it made him feel, he tells me, because
a fellow all by himself on the bank of a river shouting
"Prudence! Prudence!" is apt to give a false impression to
any passer-by who may hear him. However, he didn't have
to bother about that long, for at this point, happening to
glance at the river, he saw her body floating in it.

"Oh, dash it!" said Freddie.

Well, I mean, you couldn't say it was pleasant for him.
It put him in what you might call an invidious position.
Here he was, supposed to be looking after this kid, and
when he got home April Carroway would ask him if he had
had a jolly day and he would reply: "Topping, thanks,
except that young Prudence went and got drowned, re-
gretted by all except possibly Miss Maitland." It wouldn't
go well, and he could see it wouldn't go well, so on the
chance of a last-minute rescue he dived in. And he was
considerably surprised, on arriving at what he had supposed to be a drowning child, to discover that it was merely
the outer husk. In other words, what was floating there
was not the kid in person but only her frock. And why a
frock that had had a kid in it should suddenly have become
a kidless frock was a problem beyond him.

Another problem, which presented itself as he sloshed
ashore once more, was what the dickens he was going to
do now. The sun had gone in and a rather nippy breeze
was blowing, and it looked to him as if only a complete
change of costume could save him from pneumonia. And
as he stood there wondering where this change of costume was to come from he caught sight of that house
through the trees.

Now, in normal circs. Freddie would never dream of
calling on a bird to whom he had never been introduced

and touching him for a suit of clothes. He's scrupulously rigid on points like that and has been known to go smokeless through an entire night at the theatre rather than ask a stranger for a match. But this was a special case. He didn't hesitate. A quick burst across country, and he was at the front door, rapping the knocker and calling "I say!" And when at the end of about three minutes nobody had appeared, he came rather shrewdly to the conclusion that the place must be deserted.

Well, this, of course, fitted in quite neatly with his plans. He much preferred to nip in and help himself rather than explain everything at length to someone who might very easily be one of those goops who are not quick at grasping situations. Observing that the door was not locked, accordingly he pushed in and toddled up the stairs to the bedroom on the first floor.

Everything was fine. There was a cupboard by the bed, and in it an assortment of clothes, which left him a wide choice. He fished out a neat creation in checked tweed, located a shirt, a tie, and a sweater in the chest of drawers and, stripping off his wet things, began to dress.

As he did so, he continued to muse on this mystery of the child Prudence. He wondered what Sherlock Holmes would have made of it, or Lord Peter Wimsey, for that matter. The one thing certain was that the moment he was clothed he must buzz off and scour the countryside for her. So with all possible speed he donned the shirt, the tie and the sweater, and had just put on a pair of roomy but serviceable shoes when his eye, roving aimlessly about the apartment, fell upon a photograph on the mantelpiece.

It represented a young man of powerful physique seated in a chair in flimsy garments. On his face was a rather noble expression, on his lap a massive silver cup, and on his hands boxing gloves. And in spite of the noble expression he had no difficulty in recognizing the face as that of his formidable acquaintance, Captain Bradbury.

And at this moment, just as he had realized that Fate, after being tolerably rough with him all day, had put the lid on it by leading him into his rival's lair, he heard a sound of footsteps in the garden below. And, leaping to the window, he found his worst fears confirmed. The Captain, looking larger and tougher than ever, was coming up the gravel path to the front door. And that door, Freddie remembered with considerable emotion, he had left open.

Well, Freddie, as you know, has never been the dreamy meditative type. I would describe him as essentially the man of action. And he acted now as never before. He tells me he doubts if a chamois of the Alps, unless at the end of a most intensive spell of training, could have got down those stairs quicker than he did. He says the whole thing rather resembled an effort on the part of one of those Indian fakirs who bung their astral bodies about all over the place, going into thin air in Bombay and reassembling the parts two minutes later in Darjeeling. The result being that he reached the front door just as Captain Bradbury was coming in, and slammed it in his face. A hoarse cry, seeping through the woodwork, caused him to shoot both bolts and prop a small chair against the lower panel.

And he was just congratulating himself on having done all that man can do and handled a difficult situation with energy and tact, when a sort of scrabbling noise to the southwest came to his ears, and he realized with a sickening sinking of the heart what it means to be up against one of these Indian Army strategists, trained from early youth to do the dirty on the lawless tribes of the North-Western Frontier. With consummate military skill, Captain Brad-

bury, his advance checked at the front door, was trying to
outflank him by oozing in through the sitting-room window.

However, most fortunately it happened that whoever
washed and brushed up this house had left a mop in the
hall. It was a good outsize mop, and Freddie whisked it
up in his stride and shot into the sitting room. He arrived
just in time to see a leg coming over the sill. Then a face
came into view, and Freddie tells me that the eyes into
which he found himself gazing have kept him awake at
night ever since.

For an instant, they froze him stiff, like a snake's. Then
reason returned to her throne and, recovering himself with
a strong effort, he rammed the mop home, sending his adversary base over apex into a bed of nasturtiums. This
done, he shut the window and bolted it.

You might have thought that with a pane of glass in
between them Captain Bradbury's glare would have lost
in volume. This, Freddie tells me, was not the case. As he
had now recognized his assailant, it had become considerably above proof. It scorched Freddie like a death ray.

But the interchange of glances did not last long. These
Indian Army men do not look, they act. And it has been
well said of them that, while you may sometimes lay them
a temporary stymie, you cannot baffle them permanently.
The Captain suddenly turned and began to gallop round
the corner of the house. It was plainly his intention to resume the attack from another and less well-guarded
quarter. This, I believe, is a common manœuvre on the
North-Western Frontier. You get your Afghan shading his
eyes and looking out over the *maidan,* and then you sneak
up the *pahar* behind him and catch him bending.

This decided Freddie. He simply couldn't go on in-
definitely, leaping from spot to spot, endeavouring with

a mere mop to stem the advance of a foe as resolute as this
Bradbury. The time had come for a strategic retreat. Not
ten seconds, accordingly, after the other had disappeared,
he was wrenching the front door open.

He was taking a risk, of course. There was the possibility
that he might be walking into an ambush. But all seemed
well. The Captain had apparently genuinely gone round
to the back, and Freddie reached the gate with the comfortable feeling that in another couple of seconds he would
be out in the open and in a position to leg it away from the
danger zone.

All's well that ends well, felt Freddie.

It was at this juncture that he found that he had no
trousers on.

I need scarcely enlarge upon the agony of spirit which
this discovery caused poor old Freddie. Apart from being
the soul of modesty, he is a chap who prides himself on always being well and suitably dressed for both town and
country. In a costume which would have excited remark at
the Four Arts Ball in Paris, he writhed with shame and
embarrassment. And he was just saying: "This is the end!"
when what should he see before him but a two-seater car,
which he recognized as the property of his late host.

And in the car was a large rug.

It altered the whole aspect of affairs. From neck to waist,
you will recall, Freddie was adequately, if not neatly, clad.
The garments which he had borrowed from Captain Bradbury were a good deal too large, but at least they covered
the person. In a car with that rug over his lap his outward
appearance would be virtually that of the Well-Dressed
Man.

He did not hesitate. He had never pinched a car before,
but he did it now with all the smoothness of a seasoned
professional. Springing into the driving seat, he tucked the

rug about his knees, trod on the self-starter, and was off.

His plans were all neatly shaped. It was his intention to make straight for the Blue Lion. Arrived there, a swift dash would take him through the lobby and up the stairs to his room, where no fewer than seven pairs of trousers awaited his choice. And as the lobby was usually deserted except for the growing boy who cleaned the knives and boots, a lad who could be relied on merely to give a cheery guffaw and then dismiss the matter from his mind, he anticipated no further trouble.

But you never know. You form your schemes and run them over in your mind and you can't see a flaw in them, and then something happens out of a blue sky which dishes them completely. Scarcely had Freddie got half a mile down the road when a girlish figure leaped out of some bushes at the side, waving its arms, and he saw that it was April Carroway.

If you had told Freddie only a few hours before that a time would come when he would not be pleased to see April Carroway, he would have laughed derisively. But it was without pleasure that he looked upon her now. Nor, as he stopped the car and was enabled to make a closer inspection of the girl, did it seem as if she were pleased to see him. Why this should be so he could not imagine, but beyond a question she was not looking chummy. Her face was set, and there was an odd, stony expression in her eyes.

"Oh, hullo!" said Freddie. "So you got away from your lunch party all right."

"Yes."

Freddie braced himself to break the bad news. The whole subject of the kid Prudence and her myserious disappearance was one on which he would have preferred not to touch, but obviously it had to be done. I mean, you can't go about the place mislaying girls' sisters and just not mention it. He coughed.

"I say," he said, "a rather rummy thing has occurred. Odd, you might call it. With the best intentions in the world, I seem to have lost your sister Prudence."

"So I gathered. Well, I've found her."

"Eh?"

At this moment, a disembodied voice suddenly came from inside one of the bushes, causing Freddie to shoot a full two inches out of his seat. He tells me he remembered a similar experience having happened to Moses in the Wilderness, and he wondered if the prophet had taken it as big as he had done.

"I'm in here!"

Freddie gaped.

"Was that Prudence?" he gurgled.

"That was Prudence," said April coldly.

"But what's she doing there?"

"She is obliged to remain in those bushes, because she has nothing on."

"Nothing on? No particular engagements, you mean?"

"I mean no clothes. The horse kicked hers into the river."

Freddie blinked. He could make nothing of this.

"A horse kicked the clothes off her?"

"It didn't kick them off me," said the voice. "They were lying on the bank in a neat bundle. Miss Maitland always taught us to be neat with our clothes. You see, I was playing Lady Godiva, as you advised me to."

Freddie clutched at his brow. He might have known, he told himself, that the moment he dropped off for a few minutes' refreshing sleep this ghastly kid would be up to something frightful. And he might also have known, he reflected, that she would put the blame on him. He had studied Woman, and he knew that when Woman gets into a tight place her first act is to shovel the blame off onto the nearest male.

"When did I ever advise you to play Lady Godiva?"

"You told me I couldn't go wrong in imitating any of Tennyson's heroines."

"You appear to have encouraged her and excited her imagination," said April, giving him a look which, while it was of a different calibre from Captain Bradbury's, was almost as unpleasant to run up against. "I can't blame the poor child for being carried away."

Freddie did another spot of brow-clutching. No wooer, he knew, makes any real progress with the girl he loves by encouraging her young sister to ride horses about the countryside in the nude.

"But dash it——"

"Well, we need not go into that now. The point is that she is in those bushes with only a small piece of sacking over her, and is likely to catch cold. Perhaps you will be kind enough to drive her home?"

"Oh, rather. Of course. Certainly."

"And put that rug over her," said April Carroway. "It may save her from a bad chill."

The world reeled about Freddie. The voice of a donkey braying in a neighbouring meadow seemed like the mocking laughter of demons. The summer breeze was still murmuring through the treetops, and birds still twittered in the hedgerows, but he did not hear them.

He swallowed a couple of times.

"I'm sorry . . ."

April Carroway was staring at him incredulously. It was as if she could not believe her ears.

"You don't mean to say that you refuse to give up your rug to a child who is sneezing already?"

"I'm sorry . . ."

"Do you realize . . ."

"I'm sorry . . . Cannot relinquish rug . . . Rheumatism . . . Bad . . . In the knee joints . . . Doctor's orders . . ."

"Mr. Widgeon," said April Carroway imperiously, "give me that rug immediately!"

An infinite sadness came into Frederick Widgeon's eyes. He gave the girl one long, sorrowful look—a look in which remorse, apology and a lifelong devotion were nicely blended. Then, without a word, he put the clutch in and drove on, out into the sunset.

Somewhere on the outskirts of Wibbleton-in-the-Vale, when the dusk was falling and the air was fragrant with the evening dew, he managed to sneak a pair of trousers from a scarecrow in a field. Clad in these, he drove to London. He is now living down in the suburbs somewhere, trying to grow a beard in order to foil possible pursuit from Captain Bradbury.

And what he told me to say was that, if anybody cares to have an only slightly soiled copy of the works of Alfred, Lord Tennyson, at a sacrifice price, he is in the market. Not only has he taken an odd dislike to this particular poet, but he had a letter from April Carroway this morning, the contents of which have solidified his conviction that the volume to which I allude is of no further use to its owner.